IXL MATH WORKBOOK

THE ULTIMATE
THIRD GRADE
MATH WORKBOOK

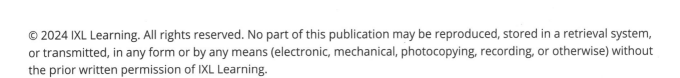

© 2024 IXL Learning. All rights reserved. No part of this publication may be reproduced, stored in a retrieval system, or transmitted, in any form or by any means (electronic, mechanical, photocopying, recording, or otherwise) without the prior written permission of IXL Learning.

ISBN: 9781947569508
28 27 26 25 24 11 12 13 14 15

Printed in China

Let's Learn!

Numbers are made up of **digits**. The value of each digit depends on its **place**. You can use a place value chart to see the places of each digit in a number. For example, look at the chart for 5,134.

Thousands		Hundreds	Tens	Ones
5	,	1	3	4

Circle the digit in the tens place.

②6   3 4   5 5 0   6 1   3 2 5

Circle the digit in the hundreds place.

2,①6 7   6, 0 9 9   4 3 7   8 4 2   2, 2 0 1

Circle the digit in the thousands place.

③,4 9 4   5, 7 2 1   5 0, 9 9 8   6, 6 7 2   7 8, 1 3 4

IXL.com skill ID

GEV

For more practice, visit IXL.com or the IXL mobile app and enter this code in the search bar.

Let's Learn!

You can use a place value chart to compare numbers. Let's try it with 2,304 and 2,172. Compare each digit from left to right.

Thousands		Hundreds	Tens	Ones
2	,	3	0	4
2	,	1	7	2

The digits in the thousands place are the same, so move to the hundreds place. Since 3 is bigger than 1, then 2,304 must be bigger than 2,172.

Circle the bigger number in each pair.

97   (397)   1,942   942

276   76   999   1,000

635   563   2,643   2,346

Circle the biggest number in each group.

768   (867)   687

390   329   392

5,372   5,237   5,273

IXL.com
skill ID
56H

Put each group of numbers in order from smallest to largest.

87	78	79		__78__	__79__	__87__	
102	92	79		_____	_____	_____	
625	621	618		_____	_____	_____	
483	473	487	478	_____	_____	_____	_____
1,008	989	994	1,012	_____	_____	_____	_____
6,514	6,451	5,614	6,145	_____	_____	_____	_____

IXL.com
skill ID
UG2

Rounding numbers

Let's Learn!

You can round numbers to any place value. Look at the digit one place to the right of the place you are rounding to. If that digit is 5 or greater, round up. Try it with 2,394.

2, 3 9 4
↓
2, 4 0 0

To round to the nearest **hundred**, look at the **tens** place.

There is a 9 in the tens place. Since 9 is greater than 5, the 3 in the hundreds place rounds up to 4. So, 2,394 rounded to the nearest hundred is 2,400.

Round each number to the nearest hundred.

528   _500_   1,374   _____   849   _____

4,909   _____   2,528   _____   962   _____

Round each number to the nearest thousand.

24,813   _25,000_   5,095   _____   2,720   _____

6,480   _____   7,399   _____   14,905   _____

41,401   _____   29,487   _____

87,622   _____   59,550   _____

IXL.com skill ID **KMD**

Add.

5 + 5 = __10__   7 + 2 = _____

7 + 6 = _____   4 + 5 = _____

9 + 6 = _____   3 + 9 = _____

10 + 4 = _____   7 + 3 = _____

6 + 8 = _____   6 + 4 = _____

8 + 3 = _____   9 + 5 = _____

2 + 9 = _____   7 + 5 = _____

7 + 7 = _____   9 + 7 = _____

Boost your math learning and save 20%!
Scan this QR code or visit www.ixl.com/workbook/3u for details.

Write the missing numbers.

4 + __7__ = 11

5 + 8 = _____

10 + 6 = _____

_____ + 10 = 20

8 + _____ = 17

9 + _____ = 13

3 + _____ = 11

_____ + 9 = 15

_____ + 10 = 19

5 + _____ = 11

6 + _____ = 13

_____ + 9 = 14

8 + _____ = 16

7 + _____ = 15

4 + 8 = _____

_____ + 6 = 14

10 + _____ = 17

_____ + 9 = 18

IXL.com
skill ID

MQX

Let's Learn!

You can use place value to add. For example, try it with 38 + 45.

$$\begin{array}{r} 1 \\ 3\,8 \\ +\,4\,5 \\ \hline 3 \end{array}$$

8 + 5 = 13

First, line up the numbers. Add the **ones**.

Remember that 13 is the same as 10 + 3. So, put the 3 in the ones column, and move the 1 to the tens column.

$$\begin{array}{r} 1 \\ 3\,8 \\ +\,4\,5 \\ \hline 8\,3 \end{array}$$

1 + 3 + 4 = 8

Now add all the **tens**.

So, 38 + 45 = 83!

Add.

$$\begin{array}{r} 1 \\ 5\,6 \\ +\,2\,6 \\ \hline 8\,2 \end{array}$$

$$\begin{array}{r} 3\,9 \\ +\,6\,2 \\ \hline \end{array}$$

$$\begin{array}{r} 2\,7 \\ +\,1\,4 \\ \hline \end{array}$$

$$\begin{array}{r} 1\,4 \\ +\,4\,5 \\ \hline \end{array}$$

$$\begin{array}{r} 6\,3 \\ +\,8\,7 \\ \hline \end{array}$$

$$\begin{array}{r} 4\,8 \\ +\,7\,6 \\ \hline \end{array}$$

Add.

$$\begin{array}{r} 3\,6 \\ +\,3\,8 \\ \hline \end{array} \qquad \begin{array}{r} 1\,3 \\ +\,7\,5 \\ \hline \end{array} \qquad \begin{array}{r} 4\,2 \\ +\,6\,6 \\ \hline \end{array}$$

$$\begin{array}{r} 5\,8 \\ +\,2\,3 \\ \hline \end{array} \qquad \begin{array}{r} 4\,0 \\ +\,8\,7 \\ \hline \end{array} \qquad \begin{array}{r} 3\,9 \\ +\,1\,1 \\ \hline \end{array}$$

$$\begin{array}{r} 6\,4 \\ +\,8\,2 \\ \hline \end{array} \qquad \begin{array}{r} 2\,3 \\ +\,5\,7 \\ \hline \end{array} \qquad \begin{array}{r} 2\,5 \\ +\,4\,8 \\ \hline \end{array}$$

$$\begin{array}{r} 5\,6 \\ +\,1\,7 \\ \hline \end{array} \qquad \begin{array}{r} 9\,4 \\ +\,8\,2 \\ \hline \end{array} \qquad \begin{array}{r} 7\,7 \\ +\,5\,9 \\ \hline \end{array}$$

TAKE ANOTHER LOOK! When you add two even numbers, what do you get? What if you add two odd numbers? What if you add an even number and an odd number?

IXL.com
skill ID
GZY

Add.

```
    5 3          4 9          7 7
    2 3          5 1          3 3
  + 6 3        + 8 7        + 2 3
```

```
    2 3          9 8          4 3
    5 8          6 1          4 9
  + 8 7        + 5 6        + 1 4
```

```
    3 4          6 1          7 3
    2 8          4 3          1 9
  + 5 0        + 3 9        + 8 2
```

Add.

```
    8 6          7 0          9 4
    6 8          1 3          9 7
    8 2          4 6          7 5
  + 2 2        + 2 2        + 8 1
```

IXL.com
skill ID
DP6

Write the missing numbers. Each number in the pyramid is the sum of the two numbers below it.

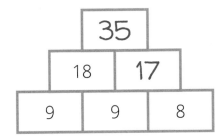

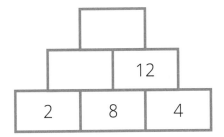

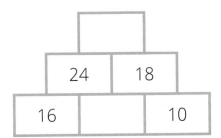

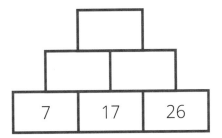

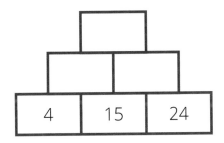

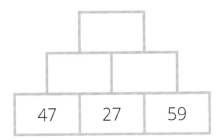

Let's Learn!

You can use place value to add larger numbers, too! Add the **ones** first, the **tens** second, and the **hundreds** last. For example, try it with 268 + 374. Remember to regroup.

$$
\begin{array}{r}
{\scriptstyle 1} \\
2\ 6\ 8 \\
+\ 3\ 7\ 4 \\
\hline
2
\end{array}
\qquad
\begin{array}{r}
{\scriptstyle 1}\ {\scriptstyle 1} \\
2\ 6\ 8 \\
+\ 3\ 7\ 4 \\
\hline
4\ 2
\end{array}
\qquad
\begin{array}{r}
{\scriptstyle 1}\ {\scriptstyle 1} \\
2\ 6\ 8 \\
+\ 3\ 7\ 4 \\
\hline
6\ 4\ 2
\end{array}
$$

8 + 4 = 12   1 + 6 + 7 = 14   1 + 2 + 3 = 6

So, 268 + 374 = 642!

Add.

$$
\begin{array}{r}
{\scriptstyle 1\ 1} \\
4\ 5\ 9 \\
+\ 2\ 5\ 6 \\
\hline
7\ 1\ 5
\end{array}
\qquad\qquad
\begin{array}{r}
1\ 6\ 8 \\
+\ 3\ 6\ 5 \\
\hline
\end{array}
\qquad\qquad
\begin{array}{r}
7\ 0\ 7 \\
+\ 2\ 8\ 5 \\
\hline
\end{array}
$$

$$
\begin{array}{r}
3\ 8\ 3 \\
+\ 6\ 0\ 4 \\
\hline
\end{array}
\qquad\qquad
\begin{array}{r}
4\ 4\ 8 \\
+\ 7\ 9\ 4 \\
\hline
\end{array}
\qquad\qquad
\begin{array}{r}
7\ 5\ 4 \\
+\ 4\ 0\ 0 \\
\hline
\end{array}
$$

Add.

$$
\begin{array}{r}
375 \\
+466 \\
\hline
\end{array}
\qquad
\begin{array}{r}
285 \\
+521 \\
\hline
\end{array}
\qquad
\begin{array}{r}
812 \\
+169 \\
\hline
\end{array}
$$

$$
\begin{array}{r}
605 \\
+326 \\
\hline
\end{array}
\qquad
\begin{array}{r}
124 \\
+747 \\
\hline
\end{array}
\qquad
\begin{array}{r}
496 \\
+275 \\
\hline
\end{array}
$$

$$
\begin{array}{r}
148 \\
+593 \\
\hline
\end{array}
\qquad
\begin{array}{r}
299 \\
+311 \\
\hline
\end{array}
\qquad
\begin{array}{r}
758 \\
+242 \\
\hline
\end{array}
$$

$$
\begin{array}{r}
619 \\
+309 \\
\hline
\end{array}
\qquad
\begin{array}{r}
154 \\
+768 \\
\hline
\end{array}
\qquad
\begin{array}{r}
482 \\
+249 \\
\hline
\end{array}
$$

IXL.com
skill ID
583

Add.

$$
\begin{array}{r}
\overset{1}{1,2\overset{}{2}4} \\
+\,1,008 \\
\hline
2,232
\end{array}
\qquad
\begin{array}{r}
8,960 \\
+\,1,363 \\
\hline
\end{array}
\qquad
\begin{array}{r}
1,735 \\
+\,4,778 \\
\hline
\end{array}
$$

$$
\begin{array}{r}
3,672 \\
+\,6,374 \\
\hline
\end{array}
\qquad
\begin{array}{r}
4,800 \\
+\,2,355 \\
\hline
\end{array}
\qquad
\begin{array}{r}
2,236 \\
+\,7,874 \\
\hline
\end{array}
$$

$$
\begin{array}{r}
9,454 \\
+\,4,828 \\
\hline
\end{array}
\qquad
\begin{array}{r}
5,307 \\
+\,6,624 \\
\hline
\end{array}
\qquad
\begin{array}{r}
1,318 \\
+\,8,097 \\
\hline
\end{array}
$$

$$
\begin{array}{r}
8,524 \\
+\,2,079 \\
\hline
\end{array}
\qquad
\begin{array}{r}
7,475 \\
+\,3,846 \\
\hline
\end{array}
\qquad
\begin{array}{r}
5,629 \\
+\,6,892 \\
\hline
\end{array}
$$

IXL.com
skill ID
P2Q

Add to complete the puzzle.

ACROSS

2. 235
     + 46

4. 489
     +602

7. 636
     + 98

DOWN

1.   24
      +54
      78

3. 3,318
      +7,763

5.   49
      +78

6.   19
      +75

IXL.com
skill ID
MH7

Answer each question.

Seaside Adventures has 96 small canoes and 25 large canoes. How many canoes does Seaside Adventures have in all?

_____ canoes

Chris and his dad both collect comic books. Chris has 87 comic books, and his dad has 346 comic books. How many comic books do they have altogether?

_____ comic books

Bella's dance teacher bought a roll of 550 scented stickers and a roll of 375 glitter stickers. How many stickers did Bella's teacher buy in all?

_____ stickers

On Thursday, the children's museum sold 453 adult tickets and 722 child tickets. How many total tickets did the museum sell on Thursday?

_____ tickets

**IXL.com
skill ID**

CNN

Home Warehouse sells gallons of paint. There are 1,459 gallons of paint out on the shelves. There are 358 gallons in the back of the store. How many gallons of paint is that in all?

_____ gallons

This picture shows the seats in Regents Theater. Use the picture to answer each question.

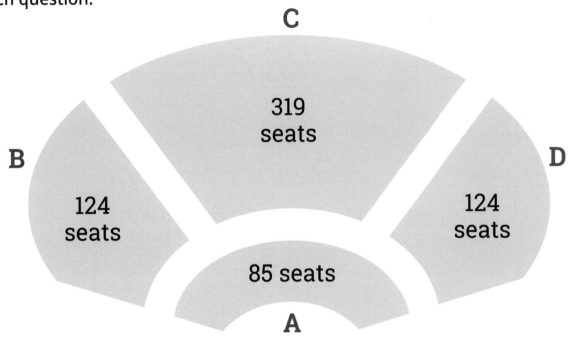

C

319
seats

B

D

124
seats

124
seats

85 seats

A

How many seats are in sections A and B?   _____ seats

How many seats are in sections C and D?   _____ seats

How many seats are in the entire theater?   _____ seats

Skylight Theater is a few blocks away. It has a total of 936 seats. How many seats are there in both theaters combined?   _____ seats

Add.

```
   1 4 4          8 3 6          5 5 5
   2 9 3          7 3 3          3 6 3
 + 4 1 6        + 4 8 7        + 1 7 9
```

```
   7, 4 1 1        8, 6 7 5
   8, 2 7 1        3, 0 9 9
 + 2, 4 5 5      + 2, 1 0 3
```

Add.

```
   2 3 4          6 5 5          5 1 3
   1 1 5          8 1 1          9 3 7
   6 4 1          6 3 2          6 1 4
 + 1 2 0        + 7 1 2        + 9 1 9
```

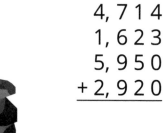

```
   4, 7 1 4        9, 3 3 9
   1, 6 2 3        1, 1 5 8
   5, 9 5 0        9, 7 0 2
 + 2, 9 2 0      + 5, 8 5 1
```

IXL.com
skill ID
X6Z

PASCAL'S TRIANGLE

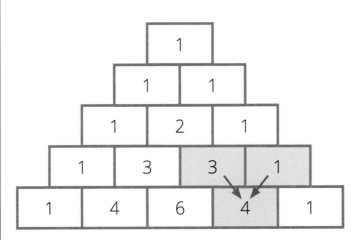

This picture shows a special triangle called **Pascal's triangle**. In this triangle, each number is the sum of the two numbers directly above it. For example, 4 equals 3 + 1.

Pick another number in the table and check. Does it follow the same pattern?

TRY IT YOURSELF!

Fill in the missing numbers.

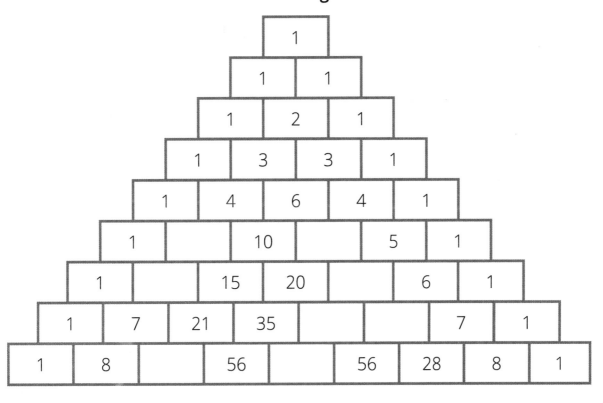

Subtract.

11 − 5 = _____   17 − 8 = _____

12 − 3 = _____   13 − 9 = _____

15 − 8 = _____   12 − 8 = _____

12 − 5 = _____   16 − 7 = _____

11 − 9 = _____   15 − 9 = _____

10 − 7 = _____   13 − 5 = _____

13 − 8 = _____   11 − 7 = _____

14 − 6 = _____   14 − 5 = _____

11 − 2 = _____   13 − 7 = _____

15 − 6 = _____   11 − 8 = _____

Write the missing numbers.

15 − 5 = _____   13 − 4 = _____   14 − _____ = 6

15 − _____ = 8   16 − 8 = _____   11 − 4 = _____

14 − 7 = _____   18 − _____ = 9   17 − 9 = _____

16 − _____ = 7   14 − 9 = _____   _____ − 6 = 10

12 − _____ = 8   11 − _____ = 5   _____ − 6 = 7

11 − _____ = 8   _____ − 10 = 10   12 − 6 = _____

For more practice, visit IXL.com or the IXL mobile app and enter this code in the search bar.

IXL.com skill ID

HSU

Let's Learn!

You can use place value to subtract. For example, try it with 53 − 27.

$$\begin{array}{r} 4\;\,13 \\ \cancel{5}\;\cancel{3} \\ -\;2\;\,7 \\ \hline 6 \end{array}$$

13 − 7 = 6

First, line up the numbers. Try to subtract the **ones**. You can't do 3 - 7! You need to regroup.

Remember that 53 is the same as 40 + 13. Cross out the 5 and write a 4. Cross out the 3 and write 13. Now you can subtract.

$$\begin{array}{r} 4\;\,13 \\ \cancel{5}\;\cancel{3} \\ -\;2\;\,7 \\ \hline 2\;\,6 \end{array}$$

4 − 2 = 2

Now subtract the **tens**.

So, 53 − 27 = 26!

Subtract.

$$\begin{array}{r} 3\;\;10 \\ \cancel{4}\cancel{0} \\ -\;2\;9 \\ \hline 1\;1 \end{array}$$

$$\begin{array}{r} 4\;4 \\ -\;3\;0 \\ \hline \end{array}$$

$$\begin{array}{r} 7\;3 \\ -\;2\;6 \\ \hline \end{array}$$

$$\begin{array}{r} 9\;6 \\ -\;2\;8 \\ \hline \end{array}$$

$$\begin{array}{r} 7\;4 \\ -\;5\;9 \\ \hline \end{array}$$

$$\begin{array}{r} 8\;3 \\ -\;6\;4 \\ \hline \end{array}$$

Subtract.

$$\begin{array}{r} 9\ 4 \\ -\ 5\ 6 \\ \hline \end{array}$$

$$\begin{array}{r} 8\ 4 \\ -\ 4\ 8 \\ \hline \end{array}$$

$$\begin{array}{r} 7\ 0 \\ -\ 5\ 4 \\ \hline \end{array}$$

$$\begin{array}{r} 3\ 7 \\ -\ 1\ 1 \\ \hline \end{array}$$

$$\begin{array}{r} 9\ 4 \\ -\ 1\ 4 \\ \hline \end{array}$$

$$\begin{array}{r} 4\ 1 \\ -\ 2\ 2 \\ \hline \end{array}$$

$$\begin{array}{r} 5\ 4 \\ -\ 1\ 5 \\ \hline \end{array}$$

$$\begin{array}{r} 6\ 2 \\ -\ 1\ 3 \\ \hline \end{array}$$

$$\begin{array}{r} 8\ 3 \\ -\ 5\ 5 \\ \hline \end{array}$$

$$\begin{array}{r} 6\ 0 \\ -\ 4\ 8 \\ \hline \end{array}$$

$$\begin{array}{r} 8\ 9 \\ -\ 7\ 8 \\ \hline \end{array}$$

$$\begin{array}{r} 9\ 1 \\ -\ 2\ 7 \\ \hline \end{array}$$

$$\begin{array}{r} 8\ 3 \\ -\ 4\ 2 \\ \hline \end{array}$$

$$\begin{array}{r} 8\ 4 \\ -\ 3\ 5 \\ \hline \end{array}$$

$$\begin{array}{r} 7\ 2 \\ -\ 6\ 8 \\ \hline \end{array}$$

IXL.com
skill ID
TWE

Subtract.

```
  9 2          4 5          6 0
- 3 8        - 2 9        - 4 1
```

```
  7 1          5 8          8 7
- 1 7        - 2 7        - 6 9
```

```
  6 4          9 5          5 0
- 1 6        - 7 9        - 2 7
```

```
  8 6          9 0          8 1
- 7 8        - 2 3        - 6 2
```

**Explore hundreds more math topics!
Get 20% off when you join IXL today.**

Scan this QR code for details.

Subtract. Follow each path!

START   FINISH

98

− 13 ↓

→ − 37

↑ − 29

FINISH

− 16 →

− 29 ↑

− 16 ←

72

START

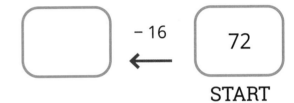

START

87   − 15 →

↓ − 28

− 28 ←

FINISH

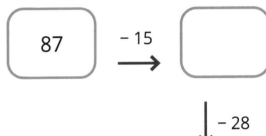

− 17 →

− 38 ↑

↓ − 27

91

START   FINISH

IXL.com
skill ID
NJ5

Let's Learn!

You can also use place value to subtract bigger numbers. For example, try it with 432 − 257.

$$\begin{array}{r} {\scriptstyle 2\;12} \\ 4\,\cancel{3}\,\cancel{2} \\ -\,2\,5\,7 \\ \hline 5 \end{array}$$

12 − 7 = 5

First, line up the numbers. Try to subtract the **ones**. You can't do 2 − 7! You need to regroup.

$$\begin{array}{r} {\scriptstyle 3\;12\;12} \\ \cancel{4}\,\cancel{3}\,\cancel{2} \\ -\,2\,5\,7 \\ \hline 7\,5 \end{array}$$

12 − 5 = 7

Now try to subtract the **tens**. You can't do 2 − 5 either! You need to regroup again.

$$\begin{array}{r} {\scriptstyle 3\;12\;12} \\ \cancel{4}\,\cancel{3}\,\cancel{2} \\ -\,2\,5\,7 \\ \hline 1\,7\,5 \end{array}$$

3 − 2 = 1

Last, subtract the **hundreds**.

So, 432 − 257 = 175!

Subtract.

$$\begin{array}{r} {\scriptstyle 8\;10} \\ 5\,\cancel{9}\,\cancel{0} \\ -\,3\,1\,1 \\ \hline 2\,7\,9 \end{array}$$

$$\begin{array}{r} 8\,7\,8 \\ -\,5\,3\,3 \\ \hline \end{array}$$

$$\begin{array}{r} 4\,7\,9 \\ -\,1\,9\,4 \\ \hline \end{array}$$

$$\begin{array}{r} 9\,2\,6 \\ -\,5\,8\,4 \\ \hline \end{array}$$

$$\begin{array}{r} 4\,1\,1 \\ -\,2\,5\,5 \\ \hline \end{array}$$

$$\begin{array}{r} 9\,4\,8 \\ -\,3\,5\,8 \\ \hline \end{array}$$

Subtract. Circle the two problems on the page that have the same answer!

$$\begin{array}{r} 754 \\ -652 \\ \hline \end{array}$$

$$\begin{array}{r} 960 \\ -467 \\ \hline \end{array}$$

$$\begin{array}{r} 922 \\ -619 \\ \hline \end{array}$$

$$\begin{array}{r} 782 \\ -694 \\ \hline \end{array}$$

$$\begin{array}{r} 510 \\ -374 \\ \hline \end{array}$$

$$\begin{array}{r} 733 \\ -163 \\ \hline \end{array}$$

$$\begin{array}{r} 934 \\ -312 \\ \hline \end{array}$$

$$\begin{array}{r} 457 \\ -392 \\ \hline \end{array}$$

$$\begin{array}{r} 762 \\ -241 \\ \hline \end{array}$$

$$\begin{array}{r} 372 \\ -164 \\ \hline \end{array}$$

$$\begin{array}{r} 751 \\ -469 \\ \hline \end{array}$$

$$\begin{array}{r} 696 \\ -576 \\ \hline \end{array}$$

$$\begin{array}{r} 544 \\ -375 \\ \hline \end{array}$$

$$\begin{array}{r} 230 \\ -201 \\ \hline \end{array}$$

$$\begin{array}{r} 574 \\ -509 \\ \hline \end{array}$$

IXL.com
skill ID
EHT

Subtract. Follow the example.

$$\begin{array}{r} {\overset{89}{\cancel{9}}}{\overset{15}{\cancel{0}}}{\cancel{5}} \\ -\ 4\ 2\ 7 \\ \hline 4\ 7\ 8 \end{array}$$

$$\begin{array}{r} 7\ 0\ 1 \\ -\ 1\ 6\ 5 \\ \hline \end{array}$$

$$\begin{array}{r} 8\ 0\ 2 \\ -\ 3\ 8\ 5 \\ \hline \end{array}$$

Subtract.

$$\begin{array}{r} 7\ 7\ 9 \\ -\ 4\ 4\ 7 \\ \hline \end{array}$$

$$\begin{array}{r} 6\ 0\ 2 \\ -\ 4\ 3\ 9 \\ \hline \end{array}$$

$$\begin{array}{r} 5\ 2\ 5 \\ -\ 4\ 7\ 1 \\ \hline \end{array}$$

$$\begin{array}{r} 5\ 1\ 8 \\ -\ 1\ 1\ 3 \\ \hline \end{array}$$

$$\begin{array}{r} 9\ 4\ 5 \\ -\ 6\ 9\ 5 \\ \hline \end{array}$$

$$\begin{array}{r} 7\ 0\ 2 \\ -\ 3\ 1\ 0 \\ \hline \end{array}$$

$$\begin{array}{r} 8\ 0\ 5 \\ -\ 7\ 2\ 3 \\ \hline \end{array}$$

$$\begin{array}{r} 8\ 3\ 1 \\ -\ 5\ 9\ 9 \\ \hline \end{array}$$

$$\begin{array}{r} 3\ 0\ 0 \\ -\ 1\ 7\ 4 \\ \hline \end{array}$$

Dive into math practice with IXL!

Get 20% off when you join IXL today.

Scan this QR code for details.

Subtract.

$$\begin{array}{r} \overset{5}{\cancel{6}},\overset{13}{\cancel{4}}\overset{12}{\cancel{2}}9 \\ -\ 4,746 \\ \hline 1,683 \end{array}$$

$$\begin{array}{r} 4,985 \\ -\ 2,366 \\ \hline \end{array}$$

$$\begin{array}{r} 9,573 \\ -\ 2,539 \\ \hline \end{array}$$

$$\begin{array}{r} 9,334 \\ -\ 8,491 \\ \hline \end{array}$$

$$\begin{array}{r} 4,968 \\ -\ 1,991 \\ \hline \end{array}$$

$$\begin{array}{r} 3,532 \\ -\ 1,578 \\ \hline \end{array}$$

$$\begin{array}{r} 2,971 \\ -\ 2,487 \\ \hline \end{array}$$

$$\begin{array}{r} 8,173 \\ -\ 7,634 \\ \hline \end{array}$$

$$\begin{array}{r} 8,359 \\ -\ 1,614 \\ \hline \end{array}$$

$$\begin{array}{r} 6,107 \\ -\ 5,999 \\ \hline \end{array}$$

$$\begin{array}{r} 8,203 \\ -\ 1,563 \\ \hline \end{array}$$

$$\begin{array}{r} 6,005 \\ -\ 3,259 \\ \hline \end{array}$$

$$\begin{array}{r} 9,300 \\ -\ 5,043 \\ \hline \end{array}$$

$$\begin{array}{r} 8,000 \\ -\ 2,639 \\ \hline \end{array}$$

$$\begin{array}{r} 6,608 \\ -\ 4,099 \\ \hline \end{array}$$

IXL.com
skill ID
Y57

Find the row, column, or diagonal where all of the answers are the same.

6,980 − 3,882	6,861 − 3,763	8,856 − 7,878
9,549 − 1,863	7,385 − 4,287	2,583 − 1,605
3,132 − 1,805	3,103 − 1,922	5,155 − 4,177

Write the missing digits.

```
    9 3 ⑤          9 7 6          2 2 6
  - 7 3 2        - 3 ◯ 8        - ◯ 9 0
  ─────────      ─────────      ─────────
    2 0 3          6 2 8            3 6
```

```
    3 ◯ 8          ◯ 1 0          8 7 2
  - 2 7 4        - 3 0 ◯        - ◯ 9 1
  ─────────      ─────────      ─────────
      6 4          2 0 1            8 ◯
```

```
  3, 7 ◯ 9        7, 7 2 2        3, 2 5 0
  - 3, 0 6 6      - 4, ◯ 6 1      -    3 7 1
  ───────────    ───────────    ───────────
    7 3 3          3, 3 6 1        2, ◯ 7 9
```

```
  8, 3 5 ◯        4, 1 ◯ 9        8, ◯ 3 0
  - ◯, 6 8 4      - 1, 0 4 9      - 2, 7 4 4
  ───────────    ───────────    ───────────
    6, 6 7 1        ◯, 0 6 0        6, 0 8 ◯
```

```
  9, 6 6 7        ◯, 6 1 0
  - 7, 5 ◯ 4      - 8, 3 9 1
  ───────────    ───────────
  ◯, 0 8 3        1, 2 ◯ 9
```

IXL.com
skill ID
V63

Subtract to complete the puzzle.

ACROSS

1.
$$\begin{array}{r} 4\,0\,3 \\ -\,2\,5\,6 \end{array}$$

3.
$$\begin{array}{r} 1,1\,8\,7 \\ -\ \ \ 9\,3\,4 \end{array}$$

5.
$$\begin{array}{r} 9,2\,0\,6 \\ -\,1,2\,8\,5 \end{array}$$

7.
$$\begin{array}{r} 6,0\,2\,4 \\ -\,5,9\,4\,8 \end{array}$$

DOWN

2.
$$\begin{array}{r} 5\,9\,0 \\ -\,1\,0\,8 \end{array}$$

4.
$$\begin{array}{r} 7\,0\,3 \\ -\,1\,9\,6 \end{array}$$

6.
$$\begin{array}{r} 5,3\,1\,4 \\ -\,5,0\,1\,8 \end{array}$$

Answer each question.

There were 114 tomatoes in Margot's garden. A family of rabbits wandered into the garden and ate 27 of the tomatoes. How many tomatoes are in the garden now?

_____ tomatoes

Arlene won $300 in a writing contest. If she spends $13 on a new notebook, how much prize money does she have left?

_____

Eric took 282 photos on his trip to Hawaii. Of the photos, 157 are of the beach. How many are **not** of the beach?

_____ photos

A candy store had 375 sour lollipops in stock. After selling some of the lollipops, there were 196 left. How many sour lollipops did the candy store sell?

_____ lollipops

There are 2,416 students in the Glenwood Elementary School District. There are 2 schools in the district. If there are 1,249 students at the first school, how many students are at the second school?

_____ students

IXL.com
skill ID

K88

Time to review! Solve.

$$
\begin{array}{r} 63 \\ -17 \\ \hline \end{array}
\qquad
\begin{array}{r} 44 \\ +93 \\ \hline \end{array}
\qquad
\begin{array}{r} 90 \\ -67 \\ \hline \end{array}
$$

$$
\begin{array}{r} 253 \\ +\ 29 \\ \hline \end{array}
\qquad
\begin{array}{r} 171 \\ -\ 38 \\ \hline \end{array}
\qquad
\begin{array}{r} 284 \\ +\ 19 \\ \hline \end{array}
$$

$$
\begin{array}{r} 712 \\ +261 \\ \hline \end{array}
\qquad
\begin{array}{r} 750 \\ -191 \\ \hline \end{array}
\qquad
\begin{array}{r} 758 \\ +617 \\ \hline \end{array}
$$

$$
\begin{array}{r} 512 \\ -478 \\ \hline \end{array}
\qquad
\begin{array}{r} 625 \\ +324 \\ \hline \end{array}
\qquad
\begin{array}{r} 672 \\ -388 \\ \hline \end{array}
$$

$$
\begin{array}{r} 801 \\ -582 \\ \hline \end{array}
\qquad
\begin{array}{r} 832 \\ +668 \\ \hline \end{array}
\qquad
\begin{array}{r} 741 \\ -498 \\ \hline \end{array}
$$

Solve.

$$8,023 + 933$$

$$6,540 + 276$$

$$1,819 - 403$$

$$9,957 - 1,024$$

$$9,292 + 3,423$$

$$5,138 - 3,349$$

$$4,687 + 3,223$$

$$3,021 - 1,353$$

$$4,351 + 2,899$$

$$5,000 - 1,058$$

$$5,144 - 4,649$$

$$9,101 + 3,854$$

$$7,879 + 5,414$$

$$8,206 - 2,949$$

$$9,005 - 4,497$$

IXL.com
skill ID
HX2

Follow the path from start to finish.

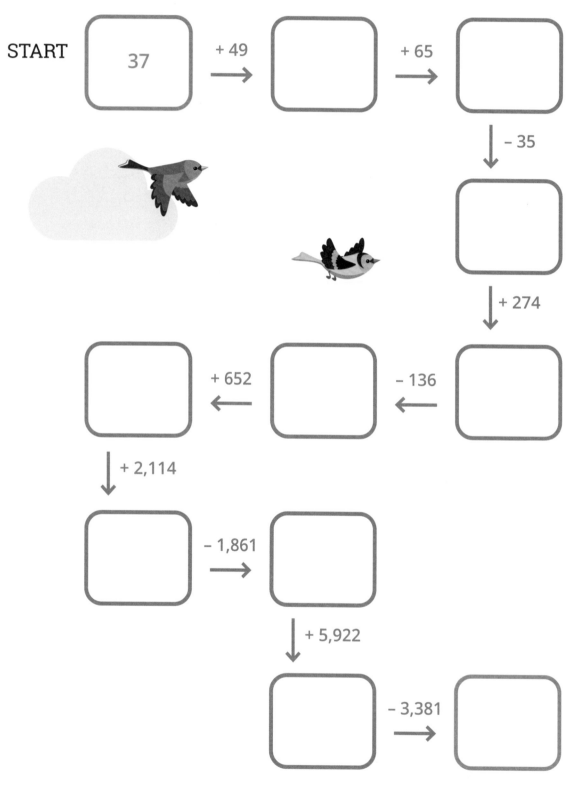

START 37   + 49 →   + 65 →

− 35

+ 274

+ 652 ←   − 136 ←

+ 2,114

− 1,861 →

+ 5,922

− 3,381 →

FINISH

Write the missing numbers. Each number in the pyramid is the sum of the two numbers below.

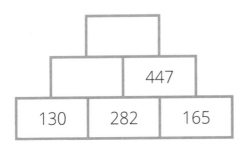

447

130 | 282 | 165

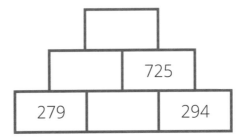

725

279 | | 294

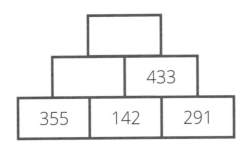

433

355 | 142 | 291

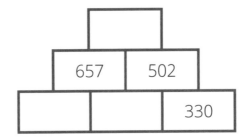

657 | 502

| | 330

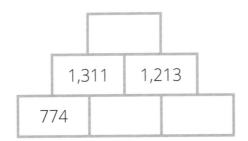

1,311 | 1,213

774 | |

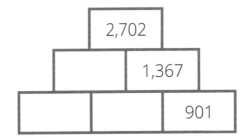

2,702

| 1,367

| | 901

20% OFF

Explore hundreds more math topics! Get 20% off when you join IXL today.

Scan the QR code for details.

Solve. Draw a line between matching answers.

1,575 − 1,325 = 250

3,447 + 1,514

263 + 424

2,435 + 1,679

592 + 336

8,542 + 4,038

9,834 − 4,873

4,187 − 3,259

505 − 255 = 250

6,730 − 2,616

7,604 + 4,976

902 − 215

IXL.com
skill ID
LSU

Fill in the blanks to make each statement true.

$352 - 219 = 33 +$ ___100___

$$\begin{array}{r} 3\,\overset{4}{\cancel{5}}\,\overset{12}{\cancel{2}} \\ -\,2\ 1\ 9 \\ \hline 1\ 3\ 3 \end{array} \qquad 133$$

$84 + 44 = 108 +$ _____

$98 - 48 = 70 -$ _____

$92 -$ _____ $= 39 + 23$

$756 -$ _____ $= 115 + 141$

_____ $+ 1{,}208 = 437 + 871$

$830 -$ _____ $= 139 + 291$

$341 + 419 =$ _____ $- 120$

_____ $- 1{,}000 = 6{,}128 - 4{,}296$

$4{,}104 + 4{,}179 =$ _____ $+ 1{,}283$

IXL.com
skill ID
5U9

Answer each question.

Alex works at Sally's Ice Pop Shop. Today, he sold 56 ice pops in the morning and 78 ice pops in the afternoon. How many ice pops did he sell?

_____ ice pops

Kelsey watched a 127-minute movie on Saturday. She watched a 98-minute movie on Sunday. How many minutes did Kelsey spend watching movies over the weekend?

_____ minutes

Ms. Miller gives her students points for cleaning the room quickly. Once the class earns 500 points, they will get a popcorn party. If the students have already earned 347 points, how many do they still need to earn the party?

_____ points

Meg's choir concert is in a big room with a main section and a balcony. There are 252 people watching the concert. If 129 of them are in the main section, how many are in the balcony?

_____ people

Marnie is a pilot. Look at her flights for this weekend. Then answer each question.

Flight	Day	Departure city	Arrival city	Flying miles
1	Sat.	New York City	San Francisco	2,586 miles
2	Sat.	San Francisco	Houston	1,635 miles
3	Sun.	Houston	Miami	964 miles
4	Sun.	Miami	Detroit	1,145 miles

How many miles is Marnie flying on Saturday?   _____ miles

How many miles is Marnie flying on Sunday?   _____ miles

How many more miles is Marnie flying on Saturday than on Sunday?   _____ miles

Next week, Marnie will fly 5,095 miles from Boston to Honolulu. How many more miles is that flight than the flight from New York City to San Francisco?   _____ miles

IXL.com
skill ID

XSH

The students in Jack's class voted for their favorite pet. This table shows the results.

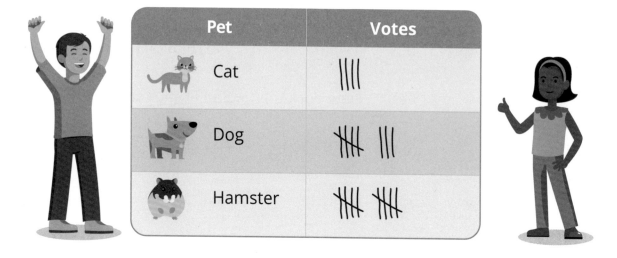

Pet	Votes
Cat	||||
Dog	ⵌ |||
Hamster	ⵌ ⵌ

Use the data in the table to complete the pictograph.

Favorite pet	
Cat	🐾 🐾
Dog	
Hamster	

Each 🐾 = 2 votes

IXL.com
skill ID
AVG

This pictograph shows the muffins that were sold at Early Bird Bakery today.

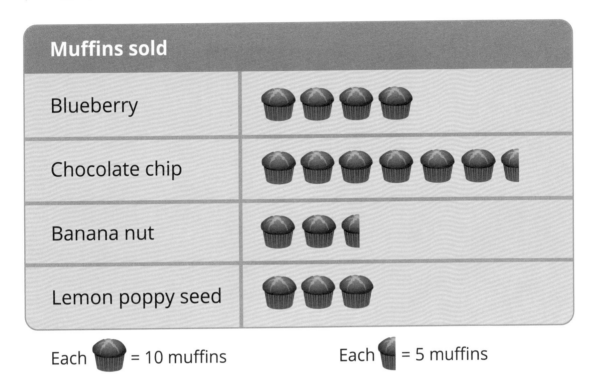

Muffins sold

Blueberry	
Chocolate chip	
Banana nut	
Lemon poppy seed	

Each = 10 muffins   Each = 5 muffins

Answer each question.

How many lemon poppy seed muffins did the bakery sell?

_____ muffins

How many more chocolate chip muffins were sold than blueberry muffins?

_____ muffins

How many banana nut muffins and chocolate chip muffins were sold?

_____ muffins

How many muffins were sold in all?

_____ muffins

IXL.com
skill ID
Y5D

This table shows the number of each type of fish in the freshwater aquarium at Lakeview Zoo.

Type of fish	Number of fish
Angelfish	30
Tetra	15
Rainbow fish	45
Swordtail	20

Use the data in the table to complete the bar graph.

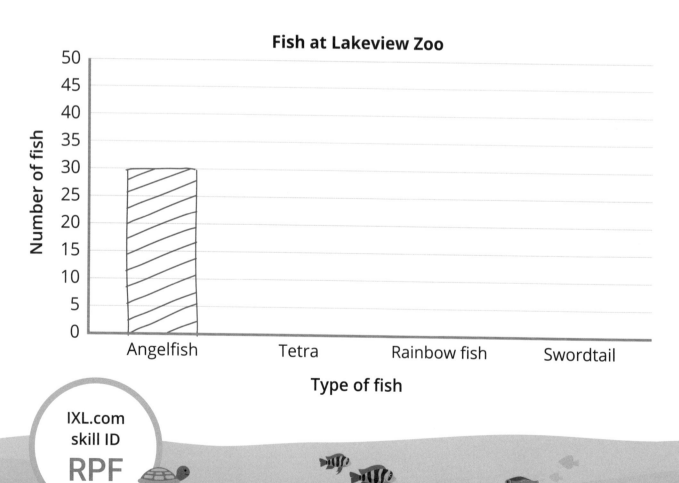

IXL.com
skill ID

RPF

Erin and her brother recorded the weather every day this past winter. This bar graph shows the results.

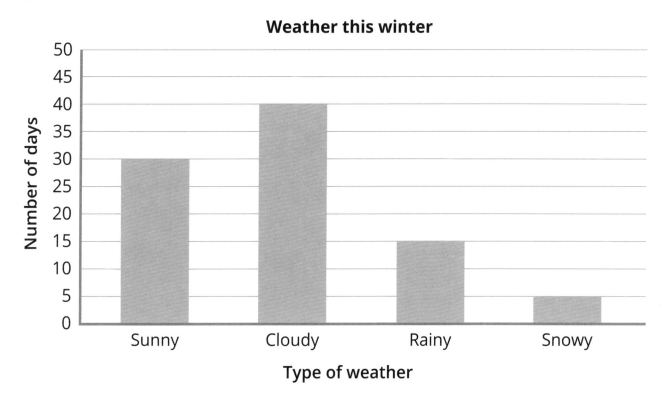

Answer each question.

How many days were rainy?   _____ days

How many more days were cloudy than sunny?   _____ days

How many more days were sunny than rainy
and snowy combined?   _____ days

For how many days did Erin and her brother
record the weather in all?

_____ days

IXL.com
skill ID
V54

Beth gives surfing lessons every Saturday. This line plot shows the number of waves each of her students surfed last Saturday.

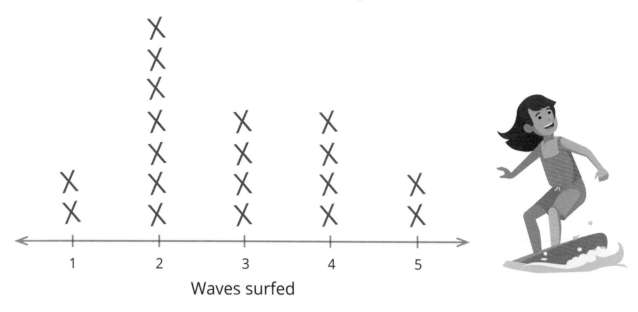

Waves surfed

Each X = 1 student

Answer each question.

How many students surfed exactly 1 wave?   _____ students

How many students surfed 3 or more waves?   _____ students

What was the highest number of waves any student surfed?   _____ waves

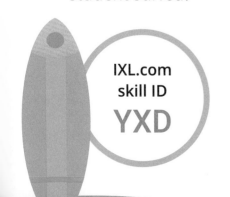

IXL.com
skill ID
YXD

What number of waves did the most students surf?   _____ waves

This table shows the height of each student in Ava's class, rounded to the nearest inch.

Height (in inches)	Number of students
52	5
53	7
54	8
55	4

Use the data in the table to complete the line plot.

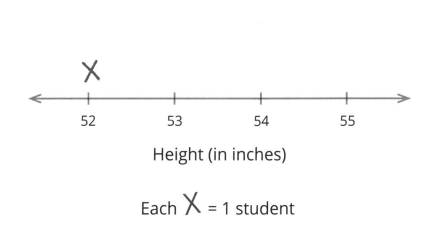

Height (in inches)

Each X = 1 student

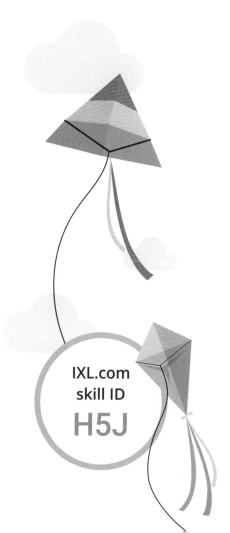

IXL.com skill ID

H5J

Get ready to multiply! Skip count to find the number of items in each group.

<u>3</u>　　　<u>6</u>　　　<u>9</u>　　　<u>12</u>　　　<u>15</u>

___　　___　　___　　___　　___

___　　___　　___　　___　　___

___　　___　　___　　___　　___

IXL.com
skill ID
LQM

For more practice, visit IXL.com or the IXL mobile app and enter this code in the search bar.

If you have equal groups, you can multiply to find the total! Fill in the blanks. Follow the example.

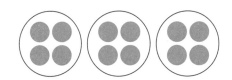

$$\underline{4} + \underline{4} + \underline{4} = \underline{12}$$
$$\underline{3} \text{ groups of } \underline{4} = \underline{12}$$
$$\underline{3} \times \underline{4} = \underline{12}$$

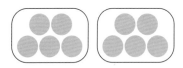

$$\underline{} + \underline{} = \underline{}$$
$$\underline{} \text{ groups of } \underline{} = \underline{}$$
$$\underline{} \times \underline{} = \underline{}$$

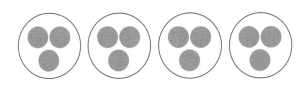

$$\underline{} + \underline{} + \underline{} + \underline{} = \underline{}$$
$$\underline{} \text{ groups of } \underline{} = \underline{}$$
$$\underline{} \times \underline{} = \underline{}$$

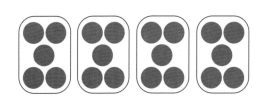

$$\underline{} + \underline{} + \underline{} + \underline{} = \underline{}$$
$$\underline{} \text{ groups of } \underline{} = \underline{}$$
$$\underline{} \times \underline{} = \underline{}$$

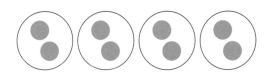

$$\underline{} + \underline{} + \underline{} + \underline{} = \underline{}$$
$$\underline{} \text{ groups of } \underline{} = \underline{}$$
$$\underline{} \times \underline{} = \underline{}$$

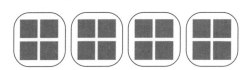

$$\underline{} + \underline{} + \underline{} + \underline{} = \underline{}$$
$$\underline{} \text{ groups of } \underline{} = \underline{}$$
$$\underline{} \times \underline{} = \underline{}$$

IXL.com
skill ID
GGC

Fill in the blanks.

How many socks are there?

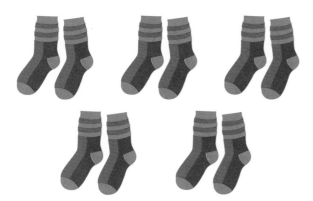

___ + ___ + ___ + ___ + ___ = ___

___ groups of ___ = ___

___ × ___ = ___

How many cherries are there?

___ + ___ + ___ + ___ + ___ = ___

___ groups of ___ = ___

___ × ___ = ___

How many books are there?

___ + ___ + ___ + ___ + ___ = ___

___ groups of ___ = ___

___ × ___ = ___

If you have equal rows, you can multiply to find the total. Fill in the blanks. Follow the example.

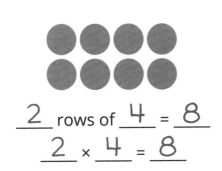

__2__ rows of __4__ = __8__

__2__ × __4__ = __8__

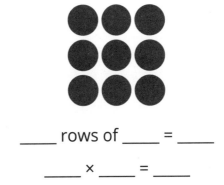

____ rows of ____ = ____

____ × ____ = ____

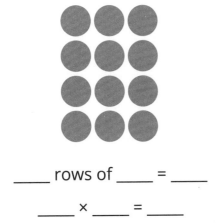

____ rows of ____ = ____

____ × ____ = ____

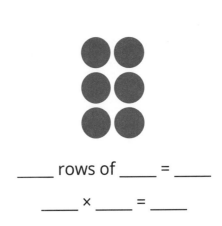

____ rows of ____ = ____

____ × ____ = ____

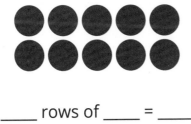

____ rows of ____ = ____

____ × ____ = ____

IXL.com
skill ID
5FZ

Fill in the blanks.

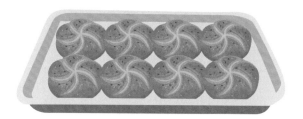

____ rows of ____ = ____

____ × ____ = ____

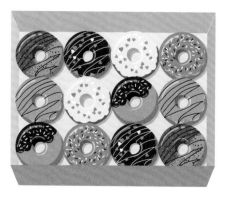

____ rows of ____ = ____

____ × ____ = ____

____ rows of ____ = ____

____ × ____ = ____

____ rows of ____ = ____

____ × ____ = ____

IXL.com
skill ID
PPR

Let's Learn!

Each number in a multiplication sentence has a special name. The numbers you multiply together are called the **factors**. The result is called the **product**.

$$4 \times 3 = 12$$

factors   product

Show off your new knowledge! Answer each question.

In 5 × 4 = 20, which number is the product? Which numbers are the factors?

Write a multiplication sentence where the factors are 2 and 3. What is the product?

Write a multiplication sentence where the product is 10 and one of the factors is 2. What is the other factor?

Write a multiplication sentence where the product is 16 and the factors are the same.

Exclusive offer! For a limited time, receive 20% off your IXL family membership.

Scan this QR code for details.

Multiply.

2 × 4 = _____   2 × 8 = _____

3 × 4 = _____   2 × 5 = _____

2 × 2 = _____   2 × 9 = _____

3 × 8 = _____   2 × 10 = _____

2 × 3 = _____   3 × 6 = _____

3 × 3 = _____   2 × 6 = _____

3 × 1 = _____   2 × 7 = _____

3 × 7 = _____   3 × 2 = _____

3 × 9 = _____   3 × 5 = _____

FIND THE PATTERN! | Look at the problems where you multiply by 2. Those answers are called **multiples** of 2. What do those answers have in common?

IXL.com
skill ID
94M

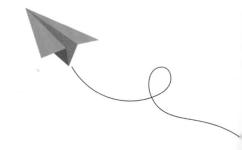

Write the missing numbers.

2 × _____ = 12   3 × 8 = _____   3 × _____ = 6

2 × _____ = 16   2 × 2 = _____   2 × _____ = 18

_____ × 10 = 30   _____ × 5 = 15   _____ × 9 = 27

2 × 7 = _____   3 × _____ = 3   2 × 3 = _____

_____ × 4 = 8   _____ × 6 = 18   2 × _____ = 2

3 × 3 = _____   3 × _____ = 21   _____ × 4 = 12

IXL.com
skill ID
38K

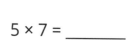

Multiply.

5 × 3 = _____

4 × 1 = _____

4 × 2 = _____

5 × 4 = _____

4 × 7 = _____

4 × 10 = _____

5 × 1 = _____

4 × 5 = _____

5 × 10 = _____

5 × 6 = _____

5 × 7 = _____

4 × 6 = _____

5 × 2 = _____

4 × 9 = _____

4 × 8 = _____

5 × 9 = _____

5 × 8 = _____

4 × 3 = _____

4 × 4 = _____

5 × 5 = _____

IXL.com
skill ID
5U6

FIND THE PATTERN! Look at the last digits of the multiples of 5. What do you notice?

Write the missing numbers.

$4 \times \underline{\hphantom{XXX}} = 40$

$\underline{\hphantom{XXX}} \times 6 = 24$

$4 \times \underline{\hphantom{XXX}} = 12$

$5 \times 5 = \underline{\hphantom{XXX}}$

$5 \times \underline{\hphantom{XXX}} = 40$

$4 \times \underline{\hphantom{XXX}} = 36$

$5 \times \underline{\hphantom{XXX}} = 35$

$4 \times \underline{\hphantom{XXX}} = 32$

$\underline{\hphantom{XXX}} \times 1 = 5$

$4 \times 4 = \underline{\hphantom{XXX}}$

$5 \times 10 = \underline{\hphantom{XXX}}$

$\underline{\hphantom{XXX}} \times 6 = 30$

$4 \times \underline{\hphantom{XXX}} = 28$

$4 \times \underline{\hphantom{XXX}} = 4$

$4 \times \underline{\hphantom{XXX}} = 20$

$\underline{\hphantom{XXX}} \times 3 = 15$

$5 \times 4 = \underline{\hphantom{XXX}}$

$5 \times 9 = \underline{\hphantom{XXX}}$

IXL.com
skill ID
Y9E

Multiply.

5 × 4 = _____

3 × 8 = _____

2 × 9 = _____

4 × 8 = _____

3 × 6 = _____

5 × 7 = _____

4 × 9 = _____

2 × 1 = _____

3 × 4 = _____

5 × 6 = _____

2 × 7 = _____

5 × 8 = _____

3 × 3 = _____

2 × 5 = _____

4 × 10 = _____

3 × 2 = _____

5 × 5 = _____

4 × 4 = _____

5 × 10 = _____

2 × 8 = _____

Multiply.

$4 \times 2 = $ _____

$3 \times 7 = $ _____

$5 \times 1 = $ _____

$3 \times 5 = $ _____

$2 \times 6 = $ _____

$4 \times 3 = $ _____

$4 \times 5 = $ _____

$3 \times 1 = $ _____

$2 \times 10 = $ _____

$4 \times 6 = $ _____

$5 \times 2 = $ _____

$5 \times 9 = $ _____

$2 \times 2 = $ _____

$3 \times 9 = $ _____

$5 \times 3 = $ _____

$3 \times 10 = $ _____

$2 \times 4 = $ _____

$4 \times 7 = $ _____

IXL.com
skill ID
DW5

Use the numbers to fill in the blanks. Use each number exactly once.

6, 8, 2, 3

_2_ × _6_ = 12

_3_ × _8_ = 24

5, 7, 4, 3

_____ × _____ = 15

_____ × _____ = 28

2, 5, 7, 4

_____ × _____ = 14

_____ × _____ = 20

9, 5, 2, 6

_____ × _____ = 18

_____ × _____ = 30

9, 4, 5, 8

_____ × _____ = 32

_____ × _____ = 45

5, 4, 8, 9

_____ × _____ = 36

_____ × _____ = 40

Find your way through the maze! Step only on stones with answers that are more than 19 but less than 31.

IXL.com
skill ID

REN

Answer each question.

Mr. McCoy just adopted 2 puppies. They each
weigh 5 pounds. How much do the puppies weigh
altogether?

_____ pounds

Jordan's class is on a field trip to the aquarium.
The students split up into 6 groups with 4 students in
each group. How many students are on the
field trip?

_____ students

A box of granola bars contains 3 different flavors.
There are 5 bars of each flavor. How many granola
bars are in the entire box?

_____ granola bars

Jack is making a bug painting in art class. He wants
to put 2 googly eyes on each bug that he paints.
If Jack paints 7 bugs, how many googly eyes will
he use?

_____ googly eyes

There are 3 packages of 6 ice cream sandwiches in
Jack's freezer. How many ice cream sandwiches are
there in all?

_____ sandwiches

Stephanie is teaching her friends how to juggle. Answer each question.

Stephanie wants to teach everyone how to juggle 3 apples at once. How many apples will she need for 7 people?

_____ apples

Stephanie, Drake, and Kevin are each juggling 4 oranges. How many oranges is that in all?

_____ oranges

Stephanie and Edwin are the best jugglers in the group. If they each juggle 5 bananas, how many bananas is that in all?

_____ bananas

Stephanie buys 5 new juggling balls. If each ball costs 10 cents, how much does she spend?

_____ cents

Multiply. Compare the products in each pair. What do you notice?

5 × 3 = _____

3 × 5 = _____

4 × 7 = _____

7 × 4 = _____

3 × 7 = _____

7 × 3 = _____

4 × 9 = _____

9 × 4 = _____

5 × 8 = _____

8 × 5 = _____

2 × 9 = _____

9 × 2 = _____

5 × 10 = _____

10 × 5 = _____

3 × 6 = _____

6 × 3 = _____

Become an IXL member
for unlimited math practice.

Scan this QR code
for details.

Multiply.

$6 \times 3 =$ _____

$6 \times 5 =$ _____

$7 \times 10 =$ _____

$7 \times 9 =$ _____

$7 \times 8 =$ _____

$6 \times 2 =$ _____

$7 \times 4 =$ _____

$7 \times 6 =$ _____

$6 \times 1 =$ _____

$7 \times 3 =$ _____

$7 \times 5 =$ _____

$6 \times 6 =$ _____

$6 \times 10 =$ _____

$6 \times 4 =$ _____

$7 \times 7 =$ _____

$7 \times 1 =$ _____

$6 \times 8 =$ _____

$6 \times 7 =$ _____

$7 \times 2 =$ _____

$6 \times 9 =$ _____

Multiply.

8 × 2 = _____   9 × 5 = _____

9 × 7 = _____   9 × 4 = _____

8 × 9 = _____   8 × 6 = _____

8 × 1 = _____   9 × 2 = _____

9 × 3 = _____   9 × 8 = _____

8 × 5 = _____   9 × 1 = _____

8 × 8 = _____   8 × 10 = _____

9 × 6 = _____   9 × 9 = _____

8 × 4 = _____   8 × 3 = _____

9 × 10 = _____   8 × 7 = _____

FIND THE PATTERN! Find the multiples of 9. Add the digits in each number. What do you get?

Multiply.

7 × 2 = _____   9 × 9 = _____   6 × 3 = _____

6 × 1 = _____   7 × 6 = _____   8 × 10 = _____

8 × 2 = _____   8 × 4 = _____   6 × 9 = _____

7 × 7 = _____   9 × 8 = _____   6 × 5 = _____

8 × 3 = _____   6 × 10 = _____   9 × 10 = _____

9 × 4 = _____   7 × 9 = _____   7 × 8 = _____

6 × 6 = _____   7 × 4 = _____   8 × 8 = _____

IXL.com
skill ID
XT7

Multiply. Draw a line to the correct answer.

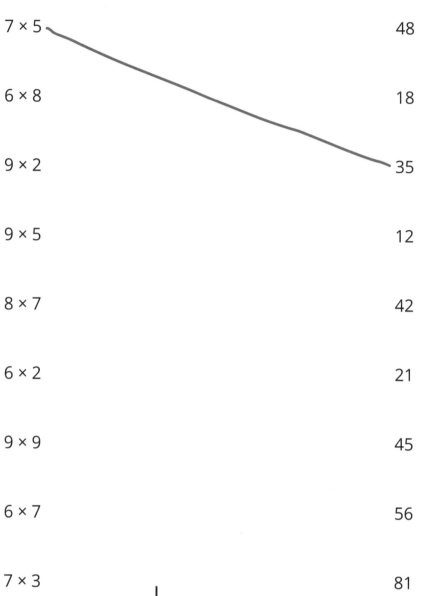

7 × 5	48
6 × 8	18
9 × 2	35
9 × 5	12
8 × 7	42
6 × 2	21
9 × 9	45
6 × 7	56
7 × 3	81

Boost your math learning and save 20%!
Scan this QR code or visit www.ixl.com/workbook/3u for details.

Write the missing numbers.

$7 \times \underline{\hspace{1cm}} = 56$ $6 \times 4 = \underline{\hspace{1cm}}$

$8 \times \underline{\hspace{1cm}} = 48$ $\underline{\hspace{1cm}} \times 5 = 40$

$\underline{\hspace{1cm}} \times 8 = 64$ $7 \times 4 = \underline{\hspace{1cm}}$

$9 \times \underline{\hspace{1cm}} = 54$ $7 \times \underline{\hspace{1cm}} = 70$

$6 \times 5 = \underline{\hspace{1cm}}$ $9 \times 3 = \underline{\hspace{1cm}}$

$\underline{\hspace{1cm}} \times 4 = 36$ $\underline{\hspace{1cm}} \times 7 = 49$

$6 \times 7 = \underline{\hspace{1cm}}$ $6 \times \underline{\hspace{1cm}} = 12$

$7 \times \underline{\hspace{1cm}} = 21$ $9 \times \underline{\hspace{1cm}} = 9$

$\underline{\hspace{1cm}} \times 7 = 63$ $\underline{\hspace{1cm}} \times 9 = 81$

IXL.com
skill ID
X7N

Answer each question.

Rico made 7 batches of cinnamon rolls.
There were 5 cinnamon rolls in each batch.
How many cinnamon rolls did Rico make?

_____ cinnamon rolls

Penny's grandmother made 7 cups of hot
chocolate. She put 8 mini marshmallows
in each cup. How many marshmallows did
Penny's grandmother use?

_____ marshmallows

Sebastian covered his notebook in wild
animal stickers. If he used 8 rows of 6
stickers, how many stickers did he use?

_____ stickers

Lucy's grandfather is turning 75 years
old. For his birthday party, there will be
6 tables with 9 people at each table.
How many people will there be?

_____ people

Answer each question.

Ryan bought a package of red, blue, and yellow modeling clay. There are 6 blocks of each color. How many blocks of modeling clay are in the package?

_____ blocks

Sally's mom bought 4 movie tickets that each cost $8. How much money did Sally's mom spend on movie tickets?

_____

Dylan's family ordered 10 sushi rolls with 6 pieces of sushi in each roll. How many pieces of sushi is that in all?

_____ pieces of sushi

Hunter has 43 pages left in his book. If he reads 8 pages a day for 5 days, will Hunter finish his book?

_____

IXL.com
skill ID
9TA

Multiply.

3 × 10 = _____

10 × 7 = _____

6 × 10 = _____

10 × 2 = _____

8 × 10 = _____

10 × 3 = _____

5 × 10 = _____

9 × 10 = _____

10 × 4 = _____

10 × 5 = _____

1 × 10 = _____

10 × 10 = _____

4 × 10 = _____

10 × 9 = _____

10 × 6 = _____

10 × 8 = _____

2 × 10 = _____

7 × 10 = _____

IXL.com
skill ID
6YD

Write the missing numbers.

$7 \times \underline{\hspace{1cm}} = 70$

$10 \times \underline{\hspace{1cm}} = 20$

$10 \times \underline{\hspace{1cm}} = 60$

$10 \times 1 = \underline{\hspace{1cm}}$

$\underline{\hspace{1cm}} \times 10 = 50$

$10 \times 10 = \underline{\hspace{1cm}}$

$\underline{\hspace{1cm}} \times 10 = 90$

$10 \times 3 = \underline{\hspace{1cm}}$

$\underline{\hspace{1cm}} \times 10 = 70$

$\underline{\hspace{1cm}} \times 10 = 60$

$10 \times \underline{\hspace{1cm}} = 80$

$\underline{\hspace{1cm}} \times 2 = 20$

$10 \times \underline{\hspace{1cm}} = 100$

$4 \times 10 = \underline{\hspace{1cm}}$

$10 \times \underline{\hspace{1cm}} = 50$

Explore hundreds more math topics!

Get 20% off when you join IXL today!

Scan this QR code for details.

MULTIPLYING BY TENS

You know 3 × 6, but how about 3 × 60? Think about another way to write the problem.

$$3 × 60 = 3 × 6 \text{ tens}$$
$$3 × 60 = 18 \text{ tens}$$
$$3 × 60 = 180$$

TRY IT YOURSELF!

Multiply.

2 × 40 = _____   6 × 20 = _____   7 × 30 = _____

3 × 30 = _____   5 × 70 = _____   4 × 30 = _____

9 × 20 = _____   3 × 80 = _____   5 × 40 = _____

6 × 50 = _____   7 × 70 = _____   4 × 80 = _____

MULTIPLYING BY HUNDREDS

Keep going! Try it with 3 × 600. Think about another way to write the problem.

3 × 600 = 3 × 6 hundreds

3 × 600 = 18 hundreds

3 × 600 = 1,800

IXL.com
skill ID
83B

TRY IT YOURSELF!

Multiply.

5 × 300 = _____   4 × 600 = _____   3 × 900 = _____

2 × 800 = _____   6 × 700 = _____   7 × 200 = _____

8 × 700 = _____   9 × 400 = _____   6 × 800 = _____

5 × 400 = _____   8 × 800 = _____   5 × 600 = _____

Exploration Zone

MULTIPLYING BY MULTIPLES OF 10

You can use patterns with zeros to multiply even larger multiples of 10. Look at the zeros in each problem. Can you find the pattern?

$3 \times 60 = 180$

$3 \times 600 = 1,800$

$3 \times 6,000 =$ _____

$3 \times 60,000 =$ _____

$3 \times 600,000 =$ _____

IXL.com
skill ID
DC9

TRY IT YOURSELF!

Multiply.

$5 \times 7,000 =$ _____

$8 \times 40,000 =$ _____

$4 \times 50,000 =$ _____

$3 \times 90,000 =$ _____

$9 \times 200,000 =$ _____

$4 \times 3,000,000 =$ _____

$9 \times 9,000,000 =$ _____

$5 \times 6,000,000 =$ _____

SOLVING PROBLEMS WITH MULTIPLES OF 10

You can use patterns with multiples of 10 to solve problems with big numbers. For example, if a factory makes 600 toy cars in an hour, how many toy cars will it make in 8 hours?

$$8 \times 600 = 4,800$$

The factory will make 4,800 toy cars in 8 hours!

TRY IT YOURSELF!

Answer each question.

The Center City Zoo is home to 3 elephants that each weigh about 8,000 pounds. What is the total weight of the elephants?

_____ pounds

The Pop Bop Bubble Gum factory makes 40,000 packs of bubble gum each day. How many packs of bubble gum does it make in 7 days?

_____ packs

It takes a team of construction workers about 200 days to build a house. How many days would it take for them to build 5 houses?

_____ days

Multiply.

6 × 4 = _____

6 × 8 = _____

5 × 5 = _____

4 × 3 = _____

10 × 8 = _____

3 × 9 = _____

3 × 5 = _____

2 × 10 = _____

2 × 7 = _____

9 × 8 = _____

8 × 2 = _____

8 × 4 = _____

7 × 3 = _____

9 × 5 = _____

7 × 6 = _____

10 × 4 = _____

6 × 5 = _____

7 × 5 = _____

8 × 8 = _____

9 × 10 = _____

IXL.com
skill ID
PNV

Multiply.

6 × 3 = _____   3 × 8 = _____   2 × 3 = _____

4 × 2 = _____   3 × 4 = _____   3 × 10 = _____

5 × 4 = _____   6 × 6 = _____   9 × 3 = _____

2 × 8 = _____   8 × 5 = _____   4 × 7 = _____

7 × 10 = _____   7 × 7 = _____   8 × 6 = _____

9 × 6 = _____   3 × 7 = _____   4 × 9 = _____

7 × 9 = _____   5 × 6 = _____   7 × 8 = _____

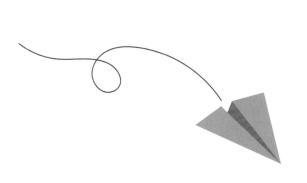

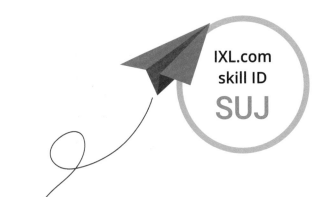

IXL.com
skill ID
SUJ

Solve each riddle.

If you multiply me by 8, you get 32. What am I?

If you multiply me by 4, you get 6 × 6. What am I?

I am a multiple of 5. I am between 6 × 2 and 4 × 4. What am I?

If you triple me, you get 21. What am I?

If you multiply me by my double, you get 50. What am I?

If you multiply me by 8, you get a number that is 2 more than 9 × 6. What am I?

Dive into math practice with IXL!
Get 20% off when you join IXL today.

Scan this QR code for details.

Ruby, Micah, Sarah, Charlie, and Zach are each different ages. Use the clues to figure out how old each person is.

Clues

- Charlie is 3 times as old as Ruby.

- Zach is twice as old as Ruby.

- Sarah is 4 times as old as Zach.

Age	Ruby	Micah	Sarah	Charlie	Zach
5					
10					
15					
20					
40					

IXL.com
skill ID
YWU

Multiply. Draw a line between the matching answers.

$8 \times 5 = 40$

3×4

5×6

9×4

2×10

8×3

4×4

9×2

3×10

6×6

$10 \times 4 = 40$

2×6

5×4

8×2

3×6

6×4

SQUARE NUMBERS

The numbers 1, 4, and 9 are all special numbers. They are called **perfect squares**. A perfect square is the product of a number times itself.

$$1 × 1 = 1 \qquad 2 × 2 = 4 \qquad 3 × 3 = 9$$

KEEP IT GOING!

You can use pictures to model perfect squares!
Fill in the missing picture.

$2 × 2 = 4$

$3 × 3 = 9$

$4 × 4 = 16$

Find the perfect squares.

$5 × 5 =$ _____ $6 × 6 =$ _____ $7 × 7 =$ _____

$8 × 8 =$ _____ $9 × 9 =$ _____ $10 × 10 =$ _____

IXL.com
skill ID
GMM

Multiply.

0 × 3 = _____

10 × 0 = _____

5 × 1 = _____

1 × 0 = _____

8 × 0 = _____

1 × 6 = _____

0 × 9 = _____

3 × 1 = _____

9 × 1 = _____

4 × 0 = _____

1 × 4 = _____

1 × 2 = _____

0 × 7 = _____

10 × 1 = _____

1 × 8 = _____

0 × 6 = _____

1 × 1 = _____

2 × 0 = _____

0 × 5 = _____

1 × 7 = _____

IXL.com
skill ID
BGK

FIND THE PATTERN! | When you multiply by 0, what do you get? How about when you multiply by 1?

Multiply.

$25 \times 1 =$ _____

$79 \times 0 =$ _____

$0 \times 98 =$ _____

$1 \times 528 =$ _____

$0 \times 654 =$ _____

$377 \times 0 =$ _____

$0 \times 710 =$ _____

$498 \times 1 =$ _____

$1 \times 5,122 =$ _____

$6,936 \times 0 =$ _____

$2,628 \times 1 =$ _____

$0 \times 4,876 =$ _____

$1 \times 7,301 =$ _____

$9,620 \times 1 =$ _____

$0 \times 5,644 =$ _____

$1 \times 9,979 =$ _____

IXL.com
skill ID
CRE

Multiply.

$11 \times 3 =$ _____

$12 \times 4 =$ _____

$12 \times 5 =$ _____

$11 \times 2 =$ _____

$12 \times 2 =$ _____

$11 \times 7 =$ _____

$11 \times 10 =$ _____

$12 \times 10 =$ _____

$12 \times 3 =$ _____

$11 \times 6 =$ _____

$12 \times 8 =$ _____

$11 \times 8 =$ _____

$11 \times 5 =$ _____

$11 \times 9 =$ _____

$11 \times 12 =$ _____

$12 \times 12 =$ _____

$12 \times 7 =$ _____

$11 \times 4 =$ _____

$12 \times 6 =$ _____

$12 \times 9 =$ _____

IXL.com
skill ID
AZJ

Write the missing numbers.

12 × _____ = 60

12 × 3 = _____

_____ × 4 = 48

12 × _____ = 96

11 × _____ = 88

_____ × 6 = 72

12 × 10 = _____

12 × _____ = 24

_____ × 9 = 99

11 × _____ = 77

11 × 11 = _____

11 × 4 = _____

12 × 7 = _____

11 × _____ = 132

_____ × 9 = 108

11 × _____ = 121

_____ × 10 = 110

12 × 11 = _____

IXL.com
skill ID
8NV

Multiply. Circle the three largest answers on the page.

8 × 9 = _____   12 × 3 = _____   1 × 10 = _____

4 × 7 = _____   11 × 2 = _____   8 × 12 = _____

5 × 12 = _____   4 × 8 = _____   5 × 11 = _____

12 × 1 = _____   9 × 9 = _____   5 × 4 = _____

6 × 7 = _____   7 × 8 = _____   8 × 6 = _____

7 × 3 = _____   7 × 10 = _____   4 × 12 = _____

5 × 6 = _____   8 × 8 = _____   9 × 4 = _____

3 × 8 = _____   6 × 6 = _____   12 × 0 = _____

IXL.com
skill ID
TK7

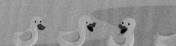

Multiply. Circle the three smallest answers on the page.

8 × 2 = _____

5 × 0 = _____

4 × 10 = _____

5 × 5 = _____

9 × 3 = _____

12 × 5 = _____

10 × 12 = _____

1 × 11 = _____

7 × 9 = _____

2 × 9 = _____

7 × 7 = _____

3 × 5 = _____

10 × 10 = _____

12 × 9 = _____

5 × 4 = _____

3 × 3 = _____

11 × 12 = _____

2 × 6 = _____

9 × 6 = _____

4 × 4 = _____

8 × 12 = _____

5 × 9 = _____

2 × 10 = _____

7 × 11 = _____

IXL.com
skill ID
YSY

Use the numbers to fill in the blanks. Do not use any number more than once.

9, 12, 7, 5

_____ × _____ = 63

_____ × _____ = 60

10, 1, 6, 5

_____ × _____ = 60

_____ × _____ = 5

0, 6, 12, 7

_____ × _____ = 0

_____ × _____ = 42

3, 6, 8, 4, 9

_____ × _____ = 18

_____ × _____ = 32

4, 8, 2, 12, 6

_____ × _____ = 48

_____ × _____ = 48

IXL.com
skill ID
VTZ

Answer each question.

Mrs. Wells bought 3 bags of sweet potatoes. There are 8 sweet potatoes in each bag. How many sweet potatoes did Mrs. Wells buy?

_____ sweet potatoes

Milo bought 6 dozen bagels. There are 12 bagels in a dozen. How many bagels did he buy?

_____ bagels

The teachers at Mountainside Elementary School set up 9 rows of 9 chairs in the gym for the school talent show. How many chairs did they set up?

_____ chairs

Ethan has $7 in quarters. How many quarters does he have?

_____ quarters

There are 8 junior league teams playing kickball on the fields at Northside Park. If there are 11 players on each team, how many players are there in all?

_____ players

IXL.com
skill ID
Z46

Let's Learn!

Sometimes you need to multiply more than two numbers together. To do that, multiply two numbers together at a time. You can use parentheses to show which pair to do first.

$$4 \times 2 \times 5 = (4 \times 2) \times 5 = 8 \times 5 = 40$$

You can group the factors in any way. You'll get the same answer each time!

$$4 \times 2 \times 5 = 4 \times (2 \times 5) = 4 \times 10 = 40$$

Show how to multiply each group of factors in two different ways.

$3 \times 2 \times 4$

$$\underline{(3 \times 2) \times 4} = \underline{6 \times 4} = \underline{24}$$

$$\underline{3 \times (2 \times 4)} = \underline{3 \times 8} = \underline{24}$$

$5 \times 2 \times 3$

$$\underline{} = \underline{} = \underline{}$$

$$\underline{} = \underline{} = \underline{}$$

$2 \times 2 \times 4$

$$\underline{} = \underline{} = \underline{}$$

$$\underline{} = \underline{} = \underline{}$$

Show how to multiply each group of factors in two different ways.

$2 \times 2 \times 1 \times 3$ $\underline{(2 \times 2) \times 1 \times 3}$ = $\underline{4 \times (1 \times 3)}$ = $\underline{4 \times 3}$ = $\underline{12}$

       _____ = _____ = _____ = _____

$3 \times 2 \times 4 \times 2$ _____ = _____ = _____ = _____

       _____ = _____ = _____ = _____

> **KEEP GOING!** See if you can come up with even more ways to solve either of the multiplication problems above.

Challenge yourself! Find the missing number.

$3 \times 3 \times \underline{\hspace{1.5cm}} = 18$ $4 \times 2 \times \underline{\hspace{1.5cm}} = 32$ $4 \times \underline{\hspace{1.5cm}} \times 3 = 36$

IXL.com
skill ID
5EC

Let's Learn!

If you know 3 × 10 and 3 × 5, then you can multiply 3 × 15, too! Look at the model below to see how.

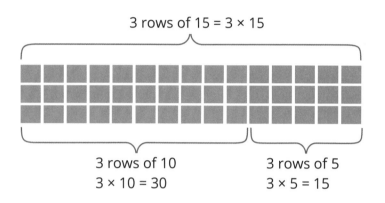

3 rows of 15 = 3 × 15

3 rows of 10
3 × 10 = 30

3 rows of 5
3 × 5 = 15

As you can see, you can split 3 × 15 into two easier problems.

3 × 15 = 3 × (10 + 5)

3 × 15 = (3 × 10) + (3 × 5)

3 × 15 = 30 + 15

3 × 15 = 45

Fill in the blanks.

To help, pick numbers that are easy to multiply, like 10.

6 × 12 = 6 × (__10__ + __2__)

6 × 12 = (6 × __10__) + (6 × __2__)

6 × 12 = __60__ + __12__

6 × 12 = __72__

7 × 16 = 7 × (_____ + _____)

7 × 16 = (7 × _____) + (7 × _____)

7 × 16 = _____ + _____

7 × 16 = _____

Fill in the blanks.

4 × 17 = 4 × (_____ + _____)

4 × 17 = (4 × _____) + (4 × _____)

4 × 17 = _____ + _____

4 × 17 = _____

8 × 23 = 8 × (_____ + _____)

8 × 23 = (8 × _____) + (8 × _____)

8 × 23 = _____ + _____

8 × 23 = _____

9 × 45 = 9 × (_____ + _____)

9 × 45 = (9 × _____) + (9 × _____)

9 × 45 = _____ + _____

9 × 45 = _____

IXL.com
skill ID
QXM

Let's Learn!

What if you want to multiply bigger numbers, like 42 × 3? Just follow these steps!

First, multiply the **ones**.

$$
\begin{array}{r}
4\ 2 \\
\times\quad 3 \\
\hline
6
\end{array}
$$

2 ones × 3 = 6 ones

Then, multiply the **tens**.

$$
\begin{array}{r}
4\ 2 \\
\times\quad 3 \\
\hline
1\ 2\ 6
\end{array}
$$

4 tens × 3 = 12 tens
12 tens = 1 hundreds and 2 tens

So, 42 × 3 is 126!

Multiply.

$$
\begin{array}{r}
5\ 3 \\
\times\ 2 \\
\hline
106
\end{array}
\qquad
\begin{array}{r}
8\ 4 \\
\times\ 2 \\
\hline
\end{array}
\qquad
\begin{array}{r}
9\ 2 \\
\times\ 3 \\
\hline
\end{array}
$$

$$
\begin{array}{r}
7\ 2 \\
\times\ 4 \\
\hline
\end{array}
\qquad
\begin{array}{r}
3\ 1 \\
\times\ 8 \\
\hline
\end{array}
\qquad
\begin{array}{r}
4\ 1 \\
\times\ 5 \\
\hline
\end{array}
$$

Multiply.

```
  3 2          4 3          9 2
×   3        ×   2        ×   4


  8 3          6 1          5 1
×   3        ×   7        ×   8


  4 2          7 2          9 1
×   4        ×   3        ×   5


  6 1          6 0          8 2
×   8        ×   3        ×   4
```

Exclusive offer!

For a limited time, receive
20% off your IXL family membership.

Scan this QR code for details.

Let's Learn!

Sometimes, you will need to regroup when you multiply. Look at 27 × 4 as an example.

First, multiply the ones.

$$\begin{array}{r} {\scriptstyle 2} \\ 2\,7 \\ \times\ \ 4 \\ \hline 8 \end{array}$$

7 ones × 4 = 28 ones

28 ones = 2 tens and 8 ones

Write the ones below. Write the tens above to save them for later.

Next, multiply the tens.

$$\begin{array}{r} {\scriptstyle 2} \\ 2\,7 \\ \times\ \ 4 \\ \hline 1\,0\,8 \end{array}$$

2 tens × 4 = 8 tens

Now add in the extra tens you saved at the top.

8 tens + 2 tens = 10 tens

10 tens = 1 hundred and 0 tens

Now read what you have left. The answer to 27 × 4 is 108!

Multiply.

$$\begin{array}{r} {\scriptstyle 4} \\ 5\,8 \\ \times\ \ 5 \\ \hline 2\,9\,0 \end{array}$$

$$\begin{array}{r} 8\,3 \\ \times\ \ 7 \\ \hline \end{array}$$

$$\begin{array}{r} 4\,4 \\ \times\ \ 8 \\ \hline \end{array}$$

$$\begin{array}{r} 2\,9 \\ \times\ \ 4 \\ \hline \end{array}$$

$$\begin{array}{r} 9\,7 \\ \times\ \ 6 \\ \hline \end{array}$$

$$\begin{array}{r} 8\,2 \\ \times\ \ 8 \\ \hline \end{array}$$

Multiply.

$$\begin{array}{r} 59 \\ \times\ 2 \\ \hline \end{array}$$

$$\begin{array}{r} 64 \\ \times\ 8 \\ \hline \end{array}$$

$$\begin{array}{r} 44 \\ \times\ 5 \\ \hline \end{array}$$

$$\begin{array}{r} 35 \\ \times\ 3 \\ \hline \end{array}$$

$$\begin{array}{r} 42 \\ \times\ 5 \\ \hline \end{array}$$

$$\begin{array}{r} 73 \\ \times\ 6 \\ \hline \end{array}$$

$$\begin{array}{r} 93 \\ \times\ 6 \\ \hline \end{array}$$

$$\begin{array}{r} 84 \\ \times\ 4 \\ \hline \end{array}$$

$$\begin{array}{r} 49 \\ \times\ 9 \\ \hline \end{array}$$

$$\begin{array}{r} 94 \\ \times\ 8 \\ \hline \end{array}$$

$$\begin{array}{r} 87 \\ \times\ 5 \\ \hline \end{array}$$

$$\begin{array}{r} 97 \\ \times\ 8 \\ \hline \end{array}$$

$$\begin{array}{r} 58 \\ \times\ 8 \\ \hline \end{array}$$

$$\begin{array}{r} 39 \\ \times\ 3 \\ \hline \end{array}$$

$$\begin{array}{r} 75 \\ \times\ 8 \\ \hline \end{array}$$

IXL.com
skill ID
9PM

Multiply.

```
  6 2          2 3          1 8
×   7        ×   4        ×   9
```

```
  5 6          5 4          3 1
×   2        ×   6        ×   9
```

```
  8 3          6 7          3 5
×   3        ×   4        ×   5
```

```
  2 8          2 9          8 6
×   6        ×   7        ×   6
```

```
  3 5          4 5          4 7
×   6        ×   9        ×   7
```

Answer each question.

Rita works at a smoothie shop. She has 4 stacks of cups with 32 cups in each stack. How many cups is that?

_____ cups

For his birthday, Elijah got $25 from each of his 4 grandparents. How much money did Elijah get in all?

_____

A mini-muffin pan fits 48 muffins. How many mini muffins can you make with 3 pans?

_____ mini muffins

There are 6 third-grade classrooms at Brian's elementary school. Each classroom has 24 students. How many third graders attend Brian's elementary school?

_____ third graders

Molly uses 64 grams of sugar to make 1 serving of cotton candy. How many grams of sugar does she need to make 8 servings of cotton candy?

_____ grams

IXL.com
skill ID
X5D

EXPONENTS

You can use a small number called an exponent to show how many times a number should be multiplied by itself. For example, in 3^2, the exponent ^{2} means that you multiply two 3s.

$$3^2 = 3 \times 3$$

In 3^3, the exponent ^{3} means that you multiply three 3s.

$$3^3 = 3 \times 3 \times 3$$

You can keep going with other exponents, too!

$$3^4 = 3 \times 3 \times 3 \times 3$$

If you see 3^2, you can say "3 squared" or "3 to the 2nd power". For 3^3, you can say "3 cubed" or "3 to the 3rd power".

TRY IT YOURSELF!

Match each exponent to what it means.

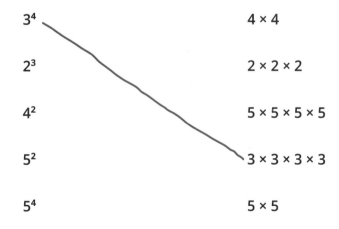

3^4	4×4
2^3	$2 \times 2 \times 2$
4^2	$5 \times 5 \times 5 \times 5$
5^2	$3 \times 3 \times 3 \times 3$
5^4	5×5

Solve.

$6^3 =$ $\underline{6 \times 6 \times 6 = 216}$ $9^2 =$ _____

$2^5 =$ _____ $5^3 =$ _____

$3^4 =$ _____ $8^2 =$ _____

$4^4 =$ _____ $7^3 =$ _____

Find the pattern! Fill in the table.

Exponents with 10			
10^2	100	2 zeros	hundred
10^3	1,000	3 zeros	thousand
10^4	10,000	4 zeros	ten thousand
10^6	1,000,000		million
10^9		9 zeros	billion
10^{12}			trillion

Follow the path from start to finish!

START | 8 | × 4 → | ☐

↓ + 49

☐ | − 74 → | ☐

↓ × 9

☐

↓ + 328

☐ | ← − 95 ← ☐ | ← − 287 ← ☐

↓ × 24

☐ | + 1,358 → | ☐ | FINISH

Solve.

$$
\begin{array}{r} 63 \\ \times\ 4 \\ \hline \end{array}
\qquad
\begin{array}{r} 53 \\ -28 \\ \hline \end{array}
\qquad
\begin{array}{r} 45 \\ +67 \\ \hline \end{array}
$$

$$
\begin{array}{r} 640 \\ -164 \\ \hline \end{array}
\qquad
\begin{array}{r} 85 \\ \times\ 7 \\ \hline \end{array}
\qquad
\begin{array}{r} 379 \\ +339 \\ \hline \end{array}
$$

$$
\begin{array}{r} 426 \\ +325 \\ \hline \end{array}
\qquad
\begin{array}{r} 605 \\ -124 \\ \hline \end{array}
\qquad
\begin{array}{r} 84 \\ \times\ 8 \\ \hline \end{array}
$$

$$
\begin{array}{r} 4,221 \\ +1,885 \\ \hline \end{array}
\qquad
\begin{array}{r} 5,320 \\ -2,866 \\ \hline \end{array}
\qquad
\begin{array}{r} 8,442 \\ -7,851 \\ \hline \end{array}
$$

$$
\begin{array}{r} 3,556 \\ +6,449 \\ \hline \end{array}
\qquad
\begin{array}{r} 92 \\ \times\ 6 \\ \hline \end{array}
\qquad
\begin{array}{r} 78 \\ \times\ 5 \\ \hline \end{array}
$$

20% off

Boost your math learning and save 20%. Join IXL today!

Scan the QR code for details.

Answer each question.

In Nikki's pantry, there are 4 full boxes of cereal bars with 6 bars in each box. She also has 2 loose cereal bars. How many cereal bars does Nikki have in all?

_____ cereal bars

Mr. Morgan has cows and goats on his farm. He has 28 cows. He has 9 fewer goats than cows. How many animals is that altogether?

_____ animals

Griffin's class is raising money for a field trip to the beach. On Monday they raised $226, and on Tuesday they raised $197. If the total cost of the field trip is $950, how much money do they have left to raise?

_____

Surf's Up Ice Cream Shop sold 97 scoops of strawberry ice cream and 248 scoops of vanilla ice cream. They sold 84 more scoops of chocolate ice cream than strawberry and vanilla combined. How many scoops of chocolate ice cream were sold?

_____ scoops

Annabelle bought 3 boxes of invitations for her birthday party. Each box of party invitations cost $6. If she paid with a $20 bill, how much change did Annabelle receive?

_____

Answer each question.

Ella is making bracelets for a craft fair. She starts with a box of 400 beads. She makes 9 bracelets with 12 beads each. How many beads are left in the box?

_____ beads

Samantha and her mom drove 456 miles to visit her grandma. On their way home, they took a different road that was 19 miles shorter. How many miles did Samantha and her mom drive in all?

_____ miles

Alex earns $5 each time he walks his neighbor's dog. He has already earned $15. If Alex wants to buy a video game for $40, how many more times will he need to walk his neighbor's dog?

_____ times

Aiden has to return his book to the library in one week. He reads 8 pages each day for 6 days. On the seventh day, he reads 5 more pages than he did on each of the other 6 days. How many pages does Aiden read in all?

_____ pages

IXL.com
skill ID
A52

Draw circles to make equal groups. Then fill in the blanks. Follow the example.

Make 2 equal groups.

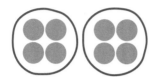

__8__ makes __2__ groups of __4__

__8__ ÷ __2__ = __4__

Make 4 equal groups.

____ makes ____ groups of ____

____ ÷ ____ = ____

Make 3 equal groups.

____ makes ____ groups of ____

____ ÷ ____ = ____

Make 2 equal groups.

____ makes ____ groups of ____

____ ÷ ____ = ____

Make 5 equal groups.

____ makes ____ groups of ____

____ ÷ ____ = ____

Make 4 equal groups.

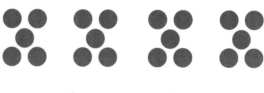

____ makes ____ groups of ____

____ ÷ ____ = ____

IXL.com
skill ID
FSX

For more practice, visit IXL.com or the IXL mobile app and enter this code in the search bar.

Fill in the blanks.

Make 3 equal groups by drawing lunchboxes around the juice boxes.

$$\underline{6} \div \underline{3} = \underline{2}$$

Make 2 equal groups by drawing nests around the birds.

$$\underline{} \div \underline{} = \underline{}$$

Make 5 equal groups by drawing mugs around the marshmallows.

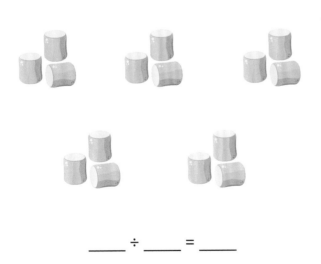

$$\underline{} \div \underline{} = \underline{}$$

Make 4 equal groups by drawing baskets around the bananas.

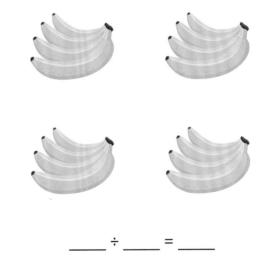

$$\underline{} \div \underline{} = \underline{}$$

Circle the rows in each model. Then write a multiplication sentence and a division sentence for each model.

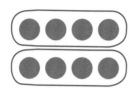

$$\frac{2}{8} \times \frac{4}{2} = \frac{8}{4}$$

_____ × _____ = _____
_____ ÷ _____ = _____

_____ × _____ = _____
_____ ÷ _____ = _____

_____ × _____ = _____
_____ ÷ _____ = _____

IXL.com
skill ID
8RW

Write a multiplication sentence or a division sentence for each model.

<u> 2 </u> × <u> 5 </u> = <u> 10 </u>

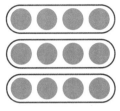

<u> 12 </u> ÷ <u> 3 </u> = <u> 4 </u>

_____ ÷ _____ = _____

_____ × _____ = _____

_____ × _____ = _____

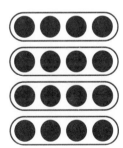

_____ ÷ _____ = _____

IXL.com
skill ID
XSK

Let's Learn!

A **fact family** is a group of math facts that use the same numbers. For example, here is the multiplication and division **fact family** for the numbers 2, 3, and 6.

$$2 \times 3 = 6 \qquad 3 \times 2 = 6 \qquad 6 \div 2 = 3 \qquad 6 \div 3 = 2$$

Use the numbers to complete each fact family.

2, 4, 8

$$\underline{2} \times \underline{4} = \underline{8}$$
$$\underline{4} \times \underline{2} = \underline{8}$$
$$\underline{8} \div \underline{2} = \underline{4}$$
$$\underline{8} \div \underline{4} = \underline{2}$$

5, 4, 20

$$\underline{} \times \underline{} = \underline{}$$
$$\underline{} \times \underline{} = \underline{}$$
$$\underline{} \div \underline{} = \underline{}$$
$$\underline{} \div \underline{} = \underline{}$$

3, 5, 15

$$\underline{} \times \underline{} = \underline{}$$
$$\underline{} \times \underline{} = \underline{}$$
$$\underline{} \div \underline{} = \underline{}$$
$$\underline{} \div \underline{} = \underline{}$$

4, 3, 12

$$\underline{} \times \underline{} = \underline{}$$
$$\underline{} \times \underline{} = \underline{}$$
$$\underline{} \div \underline{} = \underline{}$$
$$\underline{} \div \underline{} = \underline{}$$

Use the numbers to complete each fact family.

3, 7, 21

_____ × _____ = _____

_____ × _____ = _____

_____ ÷ _____ = _____

_____ ÷ _____ = _____

2, 8, 16

_____ × _____ = _____

_____ × _____ = _____

_____ ÷ _____ = _____

_____ ÷ _____ = _____

6, 2, 12

_____ × _____ = _____

_____ × _____ = _____

_____ ÷ _____ = _____

_____ ÷ _____ = _____

18, 3, 6

_____ × _____ = _____

_____ × _____ = _____

_____ ÷ _____ = _____

_____ ÷ _____ = _____

24, 6, 4

_____ × _____ = _____

_____ × _____ = _____

_____ ÷ _____ = _____

_____ ÷ _____ = _____

IXL.com
skill ID
67L

Divide.

14 ÷ 2 = _____   6 ÷ 3 = _____   2 ÷ 2 = _____

12 ÷ 3 = _____   18 ÷ 3 = _____   21 ÷ 3 = _____

6 ÷ 2 = _____   3 ÷ 3 = _____   8 ÷ 2 = _____

27 ÷ 3 = _____   12 ÷ 2 = _____   9 ÷ 3 = _____

4 ÷ 2 = _____   16 ÷ 2 = _____   30 ÷ 3 = _____

20 ÷ 2 = _____   15 ÷ 3 = _____   10 ÷ 2 = _____

Explore hundreds more math topics!
Get 20% off when you join IXL today.

Scan this QR code or visit
www.ixl.com/workbook/3u for details.

Divide.

20 ÷ 4 = _____

15 ÷ 5 = _____

36 ÷ 4 = _____

35 ÷ 5 = _____

16 ÷ 4 = _____

4 ÷ 4 = _____

50 ÷ 5 = _____

45 ÷ 5 = _____

30 ÷ 5 = _____

8 ÷ 4 = _____

10 ÷ 5 = _____

24 ÷ 4 = _____

20 ÷ 5 = _____

40 ÷ 5 = _____

12 ÷ 4 = _____

32 ÷ 4 = _____

25 ÷ 5 = _____

40 ÷ 4 = _____

IXL.com
skill ID
2JB

Divide.

$9 \div 3 =$ _____

$12 \div 4 =$ _____

$50 \div 5 =$ _____

$20 \div 2 =$ _____

$6 \div 2 =$ _____

$24 \div 3 =$ _____

$36 \div 4 =$ _____

$35 \div 5 =$ _____

$16 \div 4 =$ _____

$27 \div 3 =$ _____

$20 \div 5 =$ _____

$10 \div 2 =$ _____

$20 \div 4 =$ _____

$15 \div 3 =$ _____

$10 \div 5 =$ _____

$28 \div 4 =$ _____

$12 \div 2 =$ _____

$21 \div 3 =$ _____

$16 \div 2 =$ _____

$45 \div 5 =$ _____

Divide.

16 ÷ 4 = _____

18 ÷ 3 = _____

5 ÷ 5 = _____

14 ÷ 2 = _____

8 ÷ 4 = _____

12 ÷ 3 = _____

25 ÷ 5 = _____

24 ÷ 4 = _____

40 ÷ 4 = _____

8 ÷ 2 = _____

30 ÷ 5 = _____

18 ÷ 2 = _____

32 ÷ 4 = _____

15 ÷ 5 = _____

30 ÷ 3 = _____

40 ÷ 5 = _____

6 ÷ 3 = _____

28 ÷ 4 = _____

IXL.com
skill ID
YSD

Divide. Draw a line between the matching answers.

24 ÷ 3 = 8   40 ÷ 4

28 ÷ 4   27 ÷ 3

50 ÷ 5   16 ÷ 2 = 8

45 ÷ 5   21 ÷ 3

8 ÷ 2   16 ÷ 4

15 ÷ 5   18 ÷ 3

30 ÷ 5   9 ÷ 3

Write the missing numbers.

25 ÷ 5 = _____   12 ÷ _____ = 4

16 ÷ _____ = 4   _____ ÷ 5 = 3

21 ÷ 3 = _____   _____ ÷ 2 = 2

28 ÷ 4 = _____   35 ÷ 5 = _____

_____ ÷ 2 = 6   3 ÷ _____ = 1

20 ÷ _____ = 4   18 ÷ 3 = _____

_____ ÷ 4 = 10   24 ÷ _____ = 6

24 ÷ 3 = _____   _____ ÷ 2 = 7

IXL.com
skill ID
XDN

Answer each question.

Isabella's grandmother made 32 meatballs. She puts 4 meatballs onto each plate of pasta. If she uses all of the meatballs, how many plates of pasta is that?

_____ plates of pasta

A store sells tennis balls in cans of 3. If Jocelyn bought 18 tennis balls in all, how many cans did she buy?

_____ cans

Jeremiah picked 16 roses from his aunt's rose garden. He wants to put the same number of roses in each of 4 vases. How many roses will Jeremiah put in each vase?

_____ roses

A popcorn machine holds 50 cups of popcorn. If each small bag holds 5 cups of popcorn, how many small bags can be filled?

_____ small bags

A pet store got 18 new fish. Half are goldfish and the other half are guppies. How many fish are goldfish?

_____ fish

The sign below shows the prizes offered at Adventure Park. Answer each question about the prizes.

★ PRIZES ★

Bouncy ball	Bubbles	Sticky hand	Whistle	Slap bracelet
3 tickets	4 tickets	2 tickets	3 tickets	5 tickets

How many sticky hands can Malcolm buy with 12 tickets?

_____ sticky hands

How many whistles can Anna buy with 15 tickets?

_____ whistles

Seth has 28 tickets. How many jars of bubbles can he buy?

_____ jars of bubbles

Courtney has 32 tickets. She bought 4 bouncy balls and wants to spend the rest of her tickets on slap bracelets. How many slap bracelets can Courtney buy?

_____ slap bracelets

Let's Learn!

In a division sentence, the **dividend** is the total amount being divided up. The **divisor** is the number you divide by. The result after you divide is called the **quotient**.

$$18 \div 3 = 6$$

dividend   divisor   quotient

Answer each question.

In the division sentence 21 ÷ 3 = 7, which number is the dividend? Which number is the divisor? Which number is the quotient?

A baker divides 20 cupcakes equally into 4 boxes. She wants to know how many cupcakes will be in each box. Write the division sentence. Which number will be the dividend?

Write a division sentence where the divisor is 5 and the dividend is 30. What is the quotient?

Boost your math learning and save 20%!

Scan this QR code for details.

Let's Learn!

You can write a division problem in a couple of ways. Even though the symbols look different, they mean the same thing!

$$18 \div 2 = 9$$

dividend   divisor   quotient

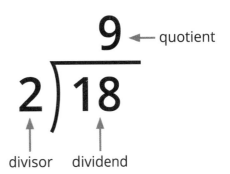

quotient

divisor   dividend

Rewrite each division sentence with the new symbol.

$$32 \div 4 = 8$$

$$12 \div 4 = 3$$

$$14 \div 2 = 7$$

$$20 \div 5 = 4$$

$$27 \div 3 = 9$$

$$25 \div 5 = 5$$

IXL.com
skill ID

E58

Divide.

14 ÷ 7 = _____   18 ÷ 6 = _____   30 ÷ 6 = _____

6 ÷ 6 = _____   35 ÷ 7 = _____   54 ÷ 6 = _____

24 ÷ 6 = _____   12 ÷ 6 = _____   7 ÷ 7 = _____

28 ÷ 7 = _____   42 ÷ 6 = _____   21 ÷ 7 = _____

6) 24   6) 36   7) 56

6) 48   7) 42   7) 63

7) 49   7) 70   6) 60

Divide.

40 ÷ 8 = _____

16 ÷ 8 = _____

27 ÷ 9 = _____

72 ÷ 9 = _____

24 ÷ 8 = _____

9 ÷ 9 = _____

90 ÷ 9 = _____

45 ÷ 9 = _____

32 ÷ 8 = _____

8 ÷ 8 = _____

18 ÷ 9 = _____

48 ÷ 8 = _____

9$\overline{)36}$

8$\overline{)56}$

9$\overline{)81}$

9$\overline{)63}$

8$\overline{)80}$

8$\overline{)32}$

8$\overline{)64}$

9$\overline{)54}$

8$\overline{)72}$

IXL.com
skill ID
U2C

Divide.

$27 \div 9 =$ _____

$18 \div 6 =$ _____

$45 \div 9 =$ _____

$28 \div 7 =$ _____

$9 \div 9 =$ _____

$30 \div 6 =$ _____

$16 \div 8 =$ _____

$42 \div 6 =$ _____

$32 \div 8 =$ _____

$54 \div 6 =$ _____

$35 \div 7 =$ _____

$12 \div 6 =$ _____

$24 \div 8 =$ _____

$40 \div 8 =$ _____

$72 \div 9 =$ _____

$24 \div 6 =$ _____

$18 \div 9 =$ _____

$21 \div 7 =$ _____

$80 \div 8 =$ _____

$14 \div 7 =$ _____

$48 \div 8 =$ _____

IXL.com
skill ID
DBB

Divide.

$7 \overline{)42}$ $6 \overline{)60}$ $7 \overline{)35}$

$6 \overline{)30}$ $8 \overline{)72}$ $9 \overline{)54}$

$9 \overline{)18}$ $7 \overline{)21}$ $8 \overline{)24}$

$6 \overline{)48}$ $9 \overline{)45}$ $8 \overline{)40}$

$7 \overline{)63}$ $7 \overline{)14}$ $9 \overline{)81}$

$9 \overline{)27}$ $6 \overline{)18}$ $7 \overline{)49}$

Divide each number by 6.

54	9
36	
18	
30	
48	
42	

Divide each number by 7.

21	3
56	
28	
35	
70	
42	

Divide each number by 8.

40	5
72	
8	
16	
24	
64	

Divide each number by 9.

90	10
18	
45	
81	
63	
36	

Find your way through the maze! Step only on stones that are equal to 4, 5, or 6.

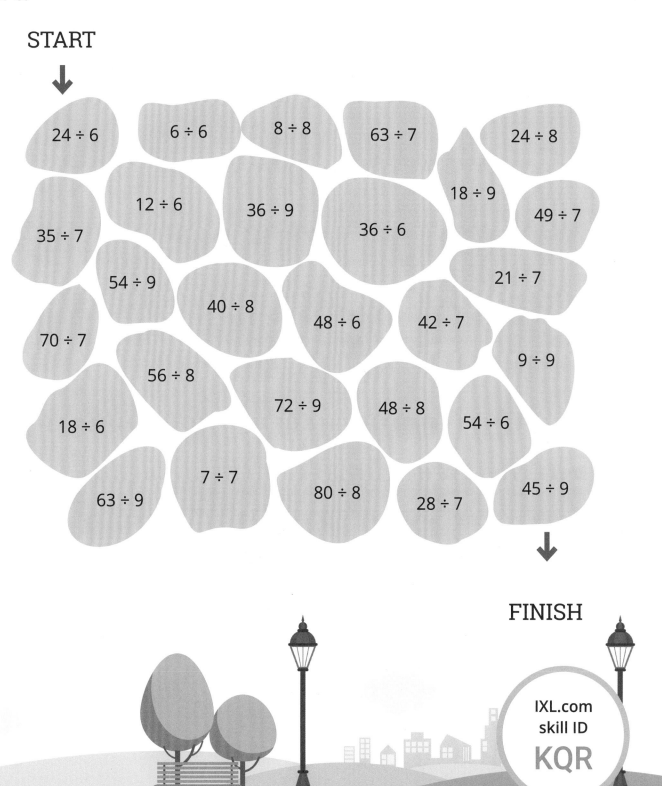

START

24 ÷ 6   6 ÷ 6   8 ÷ 8   63 ÷ 7   24 ÷ 8

12 ÷ 6   36 ÷ 9   18 ÷ 9   49 ÷ 7

35 ÷ 7   36 ÷ 6

54 ÷ 9   21 ÷ 7

40 ÷ 8   48 ÷ 6   42 ÷ 7

70 ÷ 7   9 ÷ 9

56 ÷ 8

72 ÷ 9   48 ÷ 8   54 ÷ 6

18 ÷ 6

7 ÷ 7   80 ÷ 8   45 ÷ 9

63 ÷ 9   28 ÷ 7

FINISH

IXL.com
skill ID

KQR

Answer each question.

Monty's favorite ride at the carnival is the Ferris wheel. He rode the Ferris wheel 3 times and spent 18 tickets in all. How many tickets did each ride cost?

_____ tickets

Jenna is putting 30 cupcakes onto plates for her birthday party. If there are 6 cupcakes on each plate, how many plates does Jenna use?

_____ plates

Maisey is making a quilt out of 64 squares of cloth. There will be 8 equal rows of squares. How many squares will be in each row?

_____ squares

Jake wants to save $63 to buy a new guitar. He starts washing cars in his neighborhood and charges $9 per car. How many cars will Jake need to wash to save enough money for the guitar?

_____ cars

Eliott's grandpa has 48 quarters. He gives each of his 6 grandchildren the same number of quarters. In dollars, how much money does each grandchild get?

_____

Divide.

$20 \div 10 = $ _____ $50 \div 10 = $ _____ $70 \div 10 = $ _____

$10 \overline{)\ 40}$ $10 \overline{)\ 80}$ $10 \overline{)\ 10}$

$10 \overline{)\ 90}$ $10 \overline{)\ 30}$ $10 \overline{)\ 60}$

Write the missing numbers.

_____ $\div 10 = 3$ $100 \div $ _____ $= 10$ $40 \div 10 = $ _____

$10 \overline{)\ \boxed{}}\ ^6$ $10 \overline{)\ 90}\ ^{\boxed{}}$ $\boxed{} \overline{)\ 20}\ ^2$

$10 \overline{)\ 70}\ ^{\boxed{}}$ $10 \overline{)\ 50}\ ^{\boxed{}}$ $10 \overline{)\ \boxed{}}\ ^8$

IXL.com
skill ID
YRG

DIVIDING WITH MULTIPLES OF TEN

You know 18 ÷ 3, but how about 180 ÷ 3? Think about another way to write that problem.

$$180 ÷ 3 = 18 \text{ tens} ÷ 3$$
$$180 ÷ 3 = 6 \text{ tens}$$
$$180 ÷ 3 = 60$$

IXL.com
skill ID
PTM

KEEP IT GOING!

Divide.

250 ÷ 5 = _____   240 ÷ 3 = _____   160 ÷ 2 = _____

320 ÷ 8 = _____   360 ÷ 4 = _____   720 ÷ 9 = _____

210 ÷ 7 = _____   480 ÷ 8 = _____   540 ÷ 6 = _____

270 ÷ 9 = _____   350 ÷ 5 = _____   450 ÷ 9 = _____

PATTERNS WITH MULTIPLES OF TEN

Can you solve 28,000 ÷ 4? You can use similar steps.

28,000 ÷ 4 = 28 thousands ÷ 4

28,000 ÷ 4 = 7 thousands

28,000 ÷ 4 = 7,000

Have you noticed the pattern yet? Look at the zeros to find the shortcut for dividing numbers that end in zero.

150 ÷ 5 = 30

1,500 ÷ 5 = 300

15,000 ÷ 5 = 3,000

150,000 ÷ 5 = 30,000

15,000,000 ÷ 5 = 3,000,000

IXL.com
skill ID
WRN

TRY IT YOURSELF!

Divide.

3,600 ÷ 6 = _____

1,400 ÷ 2 = _____

12,000 ÷ 4 = _____

160,000 ÷ 8 = _____

810,000 ÷ 9 = _____

30,000,000 ÷ 5 = _____

Divide.

$3 \div 1 =$ ___3___ $9 \div 1 =$ _____

$6 \div 6 =$ ___1___ $2 \div 2 =$ _____

$10 \div 1 =$ _____ $5 \div 1 =$ _____

$2 \div 1 =$ _____ $3 \div 3 =$ _____

$8 \div 8 =$ _____ $6 \div 1 =$ _____

$10 \div 10 =$ _____ $9 \div 9 =$ _____

$4 \div 4 =$ _____ $7 \div 1 =$ _____

$8 \div 1 =$ _____ $1 \div 1 =$ _____

$7 \div 7 =$ _____ $5 \div 5 =$ _____

IXL.com
skill ID
VTL

FIND THE PATTERN!   Can you come up with a rule for dividing by 1? What about for dividing a number by itself?

Divide.

$0 \div 2 =$ _O_

$0 \div 8 =$ _____

$0 \div 10 =$ _____

$0 \div 5 =$ _____

$0 \div 6 =$ _____

$0 \div 1 =$ _____

$0 \div 3 =$ _____

$0 \div 9 =$ _____

$0 \div 7 =$ _____

$0 \div 4 =$ _____

Keep it going! Divide.

$0 \div 16 =$ _____

$0 \div 28 =$ _____

$0 \div 47 =$ _____

$0 \div 93 =$ _____

Exclusive offer!

For a limited time, receive 20% off your
IXL family membership.

Scan this QR code or visit www.ixl.com/workbook/3u for details.

Divide.

24 ÷ 12 = _____   55 ÷ 11 = _____   48 ÷ 12 = _____

77 ÷ 11 = _____   72 ÷ 12 = _____   22 ÷ 11 = _____

33 ÷ 11 = _____   121 ÷ 11 = _____   96 ÷ 12 = _____

60 ÷ 12 = _____   108 ÷ 12 = _____   88 ÷ 11 = _____

$11\overline{)44}$ $11\overline{)66}$ $12\overline{)144}$

$12\overline{)36}$ $12\overline{)84}$ $11\overline{)99}$

$12\overline{)96}$ $11\overline{)110}$ $12\overline{)48}$

IXL.com
skill ID
WU9 $12\overline{)120}$ $11\overline{)33}$

Write the missing numbers.

$36 \div 12 =$ _____   _____ $\div 11 = 12$ $72 \div$ _____ $= 6$

$108 \div$ _____ $= 9$ _____ $\div 11 = 5$ $88 \div 11 =$ _____

$110 \div 11 =$ _____ $24 \div$ _____ $= 2$ _____ $\div 12 = 7$

$11 \overline{)77}$ with box above $12 \overline{)}$ with 4 above $11 \overline{)}$ with 3 above

$ \overline{)22}$ with 2 above $12 \overline{)120}$ with box above $12 \overline{)}$ with 1 above

$12 \overline{)60}$ with box above $ \overline{)44}$ with 4 above $11 \overline{)}$ with 9 above

$12 \overline{)}$ with 11 above

IXL.com
skill ID
QSY

Divide.

25 ÷ 5 = _____

21 ÷ 7 = _____

24 ÷ 3 = _____

42 ÷ 6 = _____

32 ÷ 8 = _____

15 ÷ 3 = _____

24 ÷ 4 = _____

55 ÷ 11 = _____

63 ÷ 7 = _____

30 ÷ 6 = _____

64 ÷ 8 = _____

45 ÷ 9 = _____

72 ÷ 12 = _____

16 ÷ 2 = _____

56 ÷ 7 = _____

35 ÷ 5 = _____

27 ÷ 3 = _____

36 ÷ 6 = _____

108 ÷ 12 = _____

70 ÷ 7 = _____

28 ÷ 7 = _____

IXL.com
skill ID
TA7

Divide.

$12 \overline{)132}$ $7 \overline{)42}$ $5 \overline{)20}$

$4 \overline{)28}$ $9 \overline{)81}$ $4 \overline{)32}$

$9 \overline{)72}$ $3 \overline{)21}$ $8 \overline{)40}$

$7 \overline{)49}$ $11 \overline{)121}$ $5 \overline{)50}$

$12 \overline{)96}$ $8 \overline{)56}$ $9 \overline{)54}$

IXL.com
skill ID

ZBR

Find the row, column, or diagonal where all of the quotients are the same.

24 ÷ 6	16 ÷ 4	48 ÷ 8
70 ÷ 7	40 ÷ 10	24 ÷ 2
28 ÷ 4	81 ÷ 9	32 ÷ 8

84 ÷ 12	33 ÷ 3	55 ÷ 5
56 ÷ 8	49 ÷ 7	77 ÷ 11
32 ÷ 4	56 ÷ 7	40 ÷ 4

42 ÷ 7	24 ÷ 4	20 ÷ 4
60 ÷ 12	35 ÷ 7	16 ÷ 2
40 ÷ 8	55 ÷ 11	30 ÷ 10

40 ÷ 5	30 ÷ 3	60 ÷ 12
90 ÷ 9	60 ÷ 6	20 ÷ 4
100 ÷ 10	70 ÷ 7	30 ÷ 5

36 ÷ 3	60 ÷ 5	27 ÷ 3
84 ÷ 7	72 ÷ 6	45 ÷ 5
108 ÷ 9	36 ÷ 6	48 ÷ 8

IXL.com
skill ID
YCQ

South Bay Aquarium has a cafe near the shark tank. Use the menu to answer each question.

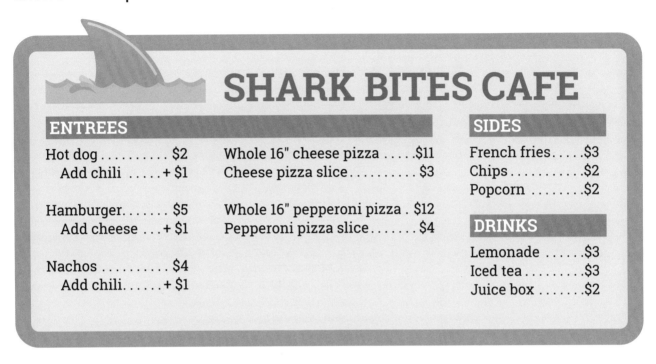

SHARK BITES CAFE

ENTREES

Hot dog $2
   Add chili . . . . . + $1

Hamburger. $5
   Add cheese . . . + $1

Nachos $4
   Add chili. . . . . . + $1

Whole 16" cheese pizza $11
Cheese pizza slice. $3

Whole 16" pepperoni pizza . $12
Pepperoni pizza slice. $4

SIDES

French fries. $3
Chips $2
Popcorn $2

DRINKS

Lemonade $3
Iced tea $3
Juice box $2

Grace's family stopped at the cafe for snacks. They spent $12 on popcorn. How many orders of popcorn did they buy?

_____ orders

Grace's family also spent $11 on several lemonades and one juice box. How many lemonades did they buy?

_____ lemonades

Two months later, Grace visited the aquarium again with her classmates. Her teacher spent $67 on pizzas. One pizza was pepperoni, and the rest were cheese. How many cheese pizzas did Grace's teacher order?

_____ cheese pizzas

IXL.com
skill ID
ECS

Solve.

3 × 5 = _____

7 × 11 = _____

33 ÷ 3 = _____

14 ÷ 7 = _____

1 × 6 = _____

4 ÷ 1 = _____

11 × 10 = _____

30 ÷ 5 = _____

7 × 8 = _____

45 ÷ 9 = _____

12 × 2 = _____

5 × 3 = _____

20 ÷ 2 = _____

30 ÷ 10 = _____

9 × 6 = _____

36 ÷ 6 = _____

8 × 6 = _____

27 ÷ 9 = _____

48 ÷ 4 = _____

3 × 7 = _____

10 × 5 = _____

32 ÷ 4 = _____

4 × 9 = _____

84 ÷ 12 = _____

Solve.

$2 \times 9 =$ _____

$35 \div 5 =$ _____

$7 \times 7 =$ _____

$48 \div 6 =$ _____

$12 \times 7 =$ _____

$9 \times 3 =$ _____

$81 \div 9 =$ _____

$5 \times 4 =$ _____

$40 \div 8 =$ _____

$8 \times 8 =$ _____

$28 \div 4 =$ _____

$36 \div 9 =$ _____

$18 \div 3 =$ _____

$12 \times 12 =$ _____

$90 \div 10 =$ _____

$5 \times 5 =$ _____

$12 \div 3 =$ _____

$6 \times 7 =$ _____

$11 \times 11 =$ _____

$8 \times 9 =$ _____

$30 \div 6 =$ _____

$16 \div 2 =$ _____

$3 \times 11 =$ _____

$16 \div 8 =$ _____

IXL.com
skill ID
UAG

Write the missing numbers.

START

6 × 4 →

÷ 12

× 10 ←

÷ 5

× 9 → ÷ 3 → × 6 →

÷ 8

× 7 ←

FINISH

IXL.com
skill ID
A8Q

Write the missing numbers.

$\underline{\hspace{2cm}} \div 6 = 11$ $24 \div 3 = \underline{\hspace{2cm}}$

$2 \times \underline{\hspace{2cm}} = 10$ $60 \div \underline{\hspace{2cm}} = 12$

$\underline{\hspace{2cm}} \times 1 = 5$ $6 \times \underline{\hspace{2cm}} = 60$

$40 \div 10 = \underline{\hspace{2cm}}$ $\underline{\hspace{2cm}} \times 3 = 6$

$7 \times \underline{\hspace{2cm}} = 77$ $\underline{\hspace{2cm}} \times 7 = 28$

$9 \times 8 = \underline{\hspace{2cm}}$ $10 \div \underline{\hspace{2cm}} = 2$

$\underline{\hspace{2cm}} \div 2 = 5$ $\underline{\hspace{2cm}} \times 8 = 96$

$4 \times 9 = \underline{\hspace{2cm}}$ $54 \div \underline{\hspace{2cm}} = 6$

$12 \div \underline{\hspace{2cm}} = 3$ $3 \times 9 = \underline{\hspace{2cm}}$

$\underline{\hspace{2cm}} \div 7 = 7$ $36 \div \underline{\hspace{2cm}} = 12$

Solve.

3 + 5 = _____

24 − 6 = _____

9 × 3 = _____

100 ÷ 10 = _____

6 × 7 = _____

9 + 12 = _____

21 − 7 = _____

45 ÷ 5 = _____

90 − 9 = _____

11 × 12 = _____

12 + 11 = _____

36 ÷ 4 = _____

64 − 8 = _____

8 × 3 = _____

5 + 6 = _____

20 ÷ 4 = _____

12 × 4 = _____

50 ÷ 10 = _____

35 + 7 = _____

32 − 8 = _____

6 × 6 = _____

27 − 9 = _____

54 ÷ 9 = _____

12 × 6 = _____

IXL.com
skill ID
7RF

Write the missing numbers.

_____ × 11 = 22

5 + _____ = 15

_____ ÷ 6 = 12

11 − 7 = _____

4 × _____ = 16

7 + 5 = _____

9 + _____ = 17

_____ − 7 = 5

18 ÷ _____ = 3

_____ × 9 = 36

49 ÷ 7 = _____

_____ − 6 = 4

6 + _____ = 12

_____ ÷ 6 = 8

3 × 3 = _____

_____ × 12 = 108

20 − _____ = 10

44 ÷ 11 = _____

45 + 9 = _____

_____ ÷ 3 = 7

18 − 2 = _____

_____ − 12 = 36

7 × 7 = _____

_____ ÷ 10 = 10

IXL.com
skill ID
N5U

Write the missing numbers.

START

50 → ÷ 5 → ☐

↓ × 7

☐ → − 6 → ☐ → ÷ 8 → ☐

↓ + 4

☐ ← − 3 ← ☐ ← + 9 ← ☐ ← × 3 ← ☐

↓ ÷ 6

☐ → + 4 → ☐ → × 9 → ☐

FINISH

IXL.com
skill ID
AZH

Solve each riddle.

The product of two numbers is 36, and the sum of these numbers is 13. What are the two numbers?

When you divide this number by 6, you get the product of 3 and 4. What is the number?

The difference of two numbers is 5, and the product of these numbers is 24. What are the two numbers?

When you multiply this number by 7, you get the difference of 42 and 28. What is the number?

The quotient of two numbers is 10, and the sum of these numbers is 55. What are the two numbers?

When you add this number to 3, you get the quotient of 48 and 6. What is the number?

The product of two numbers is 18, and one of the numbers is half of the other number. What are the two numbers?

IXL.com
skill ID
DAV

Answer each question.

Marley had 5 ten-dollar bills in his wallet. He bought a new baseball glove for $16. How much money does Marley have now?

_____

Emily can fit 12 chapter books on each shelf of her bookcase. Three of the shelves are full, and one shelf has 9 books. How many books are in Emily's bookcase?

_____ books

The students in Ms. Wilson's class earn points for teamwork. The students earned 8 points each day for 4 days. On the fifth day, the students earned 11 points. How many points did Ms. Wilson's students earn in all?

_____ points

Michael and his 3 brothers shared a pack of 24 sour gummies. They shared the gummies equally. Michael ate all but 2 of his portion. How many sour gummies did Michael eat?

_____ sour gummies

Explore hundreds more math topics!

Get 20% off when you join IXL today!

Scan this QR code for details.

This sign shows how many tickets are needed for each ride at Cloverdale's spring carnival. Use the sign to answer each question.

Bounce house	Bumper cars	Carousel	Ferris wheel
8 tickets	6 tickets	3 tickets	6 tickets

Flying swings	Fun house	Giant slide	Roller coaster
5 tickets	5 tickets	4 tickets	8 tickets

Daniel and his 2 sisters each want to ride the roller coaster. How many tickets will they need in all?

_____ tickets

Emma jumped in the bounce house while her 3 brothers drove bumper cars. How many tickets did they use in all?

_____ tickets

Evan went to the carnival with his family. His mom and dad each rode the Ferris wheel. Evan rode on the flying swings, and his sister went down the giant slide. How many tickets did they use in all?

_____ tickets

Charlotte's grandpa bought 50 tickets. He gave the same number of tickets to Charlotte and each of her 4 cousins. What is one way Charlotte could spend all of her tickets?

IXL.com
skill ID

X8W

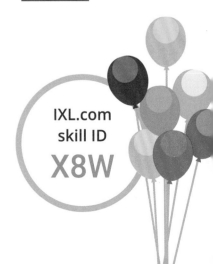

_____

Circle each shape that is split into equal parts.

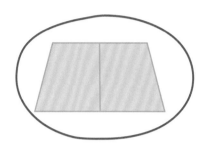  

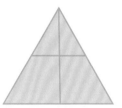  

IXL.com
skill ID
FHY

For more practice, visit IXL.com or the IXL mobile app and enter this code in the search bar.

Divide each shape into equal parts.

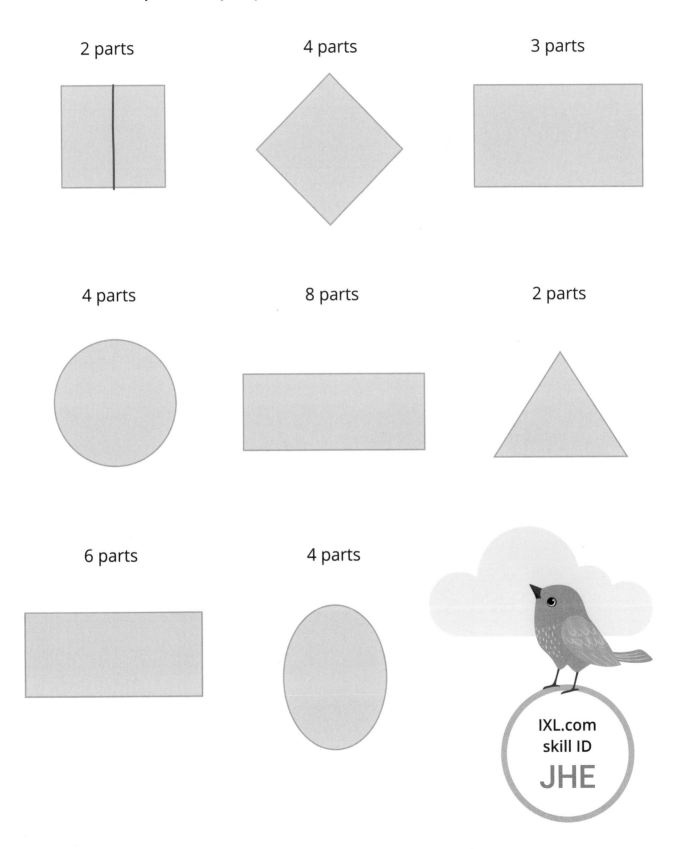

2 parts

4 parts

3 parts

4 parts

8 parts

2 parts

6 parts

4 parts

IXL.com
skill ID

JHE

Let's Learn!

There are special names for different numbers of equal parts. Here are some of those names.

Halves
Two equal parts

Thirds
Three equal parts

Fourths
Four equal parts

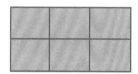 

Sixths
Six equal parts

Eighths
Eight equal parts

Write the word for the equal parts.

FOURTHS _____

_____

_____

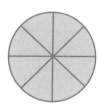  

_____

_____

_____

Let's Learn!

You can use a **fraction** to represent a part of a whole. This circle is divided into 2 equal parts, with 1 part shaded. It shows one half. Here is how to write this as a fraction:

$\frac{1}{2}$ ← number of shaded parts

← total number of parts

Write the fraction shown.

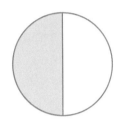 $\frac{2}{4}$

 _____

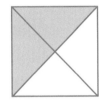 _____

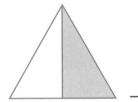 _____

 _____

 _____

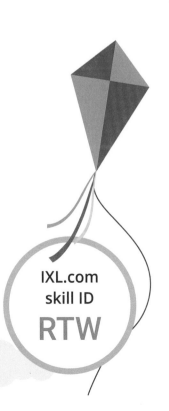

IXL.com
skill ID
RTW

Let's Learn!

You can also use fractions to show parts of a set. For example, $\frac{2}{6}$ of these jelly beans have spots.

$$\frac{2}{6}$$ ← 2 spotted jelly beans
← 6 jelly beans in all

What fraction of the cupcakes have sprinkles?

_____

What fraction of the eggs have hatched?

_____

What fraction of the fruit are apples?

_____

What fraction of the balloons are shaped like hearts?

_____

Let's Learn!

You can show fractions on number lines. This number line shows $\frac{1}{6}$.

It takes 1 jump to get to the point.

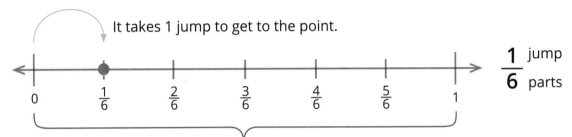

$\frac{1}{6}$ jump / parts

One whole is split into 6 equal parts.

Write the fraction shown.

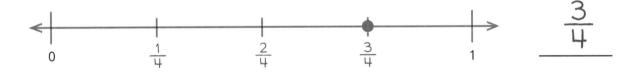

$\frac{3}{4}$

_____

_____

IXL.com
skill ID
AWH

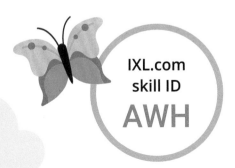

Write the fraction shown.

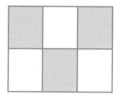

_____   _____   _____

What fraction of the mugs have a smiley face?

What fraction of the ice cream cones have melted?

What fraction of the books are open?

_____   _____   _____

Write the fraction shown.

_____

_____

Shade in each fraction.

$$\frac{3}{4}$$

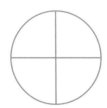

$$\frac{3}{6}$$

$$\frac{7}{8}$$

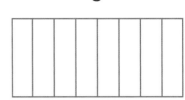

$$\frac{5}{6}$$

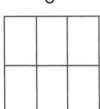

$$\frac{3}{8}$$

$$\frac{1}{4}$$

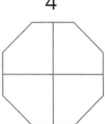

Shade in each fraction.

$$\frac{5}{6}$$

$$\frac{1}{2}$$

$$\frac{4}{8}$$

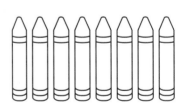

$$\frac{7}{8}$$

$$\frac{2}{6}$$

IXL.com
skill ID
ZPW

Draw each fraction.

$$\frac{4}{6}$$

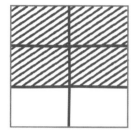

$$\frac{3}{8}$$

$$\frac{1}{2}$$

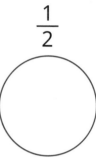

$$\frac{2}{3}$$

$$\frac{2}{4}$$

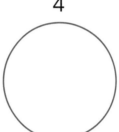

$$\frac{2}{6}$$

$$\frac{1}{4}$$

$$\frac{1}{3}$$

$$\frac{5}{8}$$

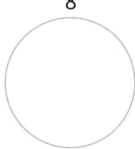

IXL.com
skill ID
NLE

$$\frac{6}{8}$$

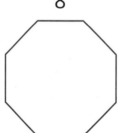

$$\frac{3}{4}$$

Show each fraction on the number line.

$\dfrac{1}{3}$

$\dfrac{2}{6}$

$\dfrac{3}{4}$

Show each fraction on the number line.

$\dfrac{1}{2}$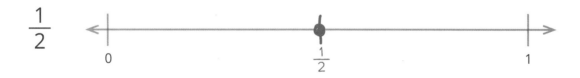

$\dfrac{2}{3}$

$\dfrac{4}{6}$

IXL.com
skill ID
7QM

Let's Learn!

In a fraction, the top number is called the **numerator**. The bottom number is called the **denominator**.

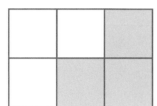

In this rectangle, 3 out of the 6 total parts are shaded. So, the numerator is 3. The denominator is 6.

$$\frac{3}{6}$$ ← numerator
← denominator

Write each fraction. Then create a model for that fraction.

A fraction with a numerator of 5 and a denominator of 6

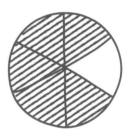

A fraction with a denominator of 4 and a numerator of 1

_____

A fraction with a numerator that is half the denominator

_____

A fraction with a numerator that is 1 less than the denominator

_____

Answer each question.

A pizza has 8 slices. If 4 of the slices have mushrooms, what fraction of the pizza slices have mushrooms?

_____

There are 8 rooms in Emma's house. If 3 of the rooms are bedrooms, what fraction of the rooms are bedrooms?

_____

Brayden's mom bought a box of 6 granola bars. Brayden ate 4 of them. What fraction of the granola bars remain?

_____

Leah has 1 cat and 2 dogs. What fraction of Leah's pets are dogs?

_____

Caleb made 1 candy apple and 3 caramel apples. What fraction of the apples have caramel?

_____

IXL.com
skill ID
Z65

Let's Learn!

You can use a fraction to show one whole, or 1.

For example, this shape has three equal parts. All three parts are shaded, so it shows $\frac{3}{3}$.

Write the fraction for each shaded model.

$\frac{4}{4}$

_____

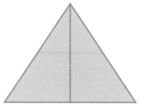

_____

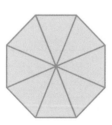

_____

_____

| **FIND THE PATTERN!** | For each fraction on the page, divide the numerator by the denominator. What number do you get? |

Let's Learn!

When you have two fractions with the same denominator, they have the same number of total parts. You can compare the numerators to see which fraction is bigger. The numerators will tell you which fraction has more of the parts shaded.

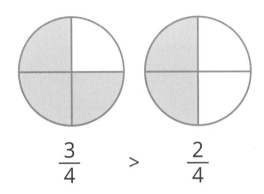

$$\frac{3}{4} \quad > \quad \frac{2}{4}$$

Compare each pair of fractions. Fill in each circle with >, <, or =.

$$\frac{1}{3} \;\bigcirc\!\!\!< \; \frac{2}{3} \qquad\qquad \frac{3}{6} \;\bigcirc\; \frac{5}{6} \qquad\qquad \frac{7}{8} \;\bigcirc\; \frac{3}{8}$$

$$\frac{2}{4} \;\bigcirc\; \frac{2}{4} \qquad\qquad \frac{1}{6} \;\bigcirc\; \frac{2}{6} \qquad\qquad \frac{2}{8} \;\bigcirc\; \frac{5}{8}$$

$$\frac{1}{4} \;\bigcirc\; \frac{2}{4} \qquad\qquad \frac{5}{6} \;\bigcirc\; \frac{4}{6} \qquad\qquad \frac{3}{4} \;\bigcirc\; \frac{1}{4}$$

IXL.com
skill ID
HYZ

Let's Learn!

A **unit fraction** is a fraction with a numerator of 1. You can compare unit fractions by looking at the denominators. The larger the denominator, the smaller the fraction.

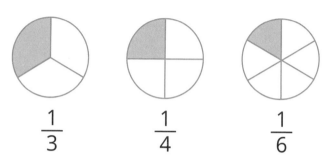

$$\frac{1}{3} \qquad \frac{1}{4} \qquad \frac{1}{6}$$

Compare each pair of fractions. Fill in each circle with >, <, or =.

$$\frac{1}{8} \enspace \boxed{<} \enspace \frac{1}{3} \qquad\qquad \frac{1}{2} \enspace \bigcirc \enspace \frac{1}{4}$$

$$\frac{1}{4} \enspace \bigcirc \enspace \frac{1}{3} \qquad\qquad \frac{1}{3} \enspace \bigcirc \enspace \frac{1}{6}$$

$$\frac{1}{6} \enspace \bigcirc \enspace \frac{1}{8} \qquad\qquad \frac{1}{6} \enspace \bigcirc \enspace \frac{1}{4}$$

$$\frac{1}{8} \enspace \bigcirc \enspace \frac{1}{2} \qquad\qquad \frac{1}{4} \enspace \bigcirc \enspace \frac{1}{8}$$

Let's Learn!

You can use the rule for comparing unit fractions to compare other fractions, too. For example, think about $\frac{2}{6}$ and $\frac{2}{3}$. They have the same number of shaded parts, but thirds are bigger than sixths. So, $\frac{2}{3}$ must be greater than $\frac{2}{6}$.

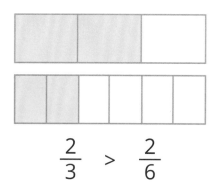

$$\frac{2}{3} \; > \; \frac{2}{6}$$

Compare each pair of fractions. Fill in each circle with >, <, or =.

$\frac{3}{8}$ ⬤< $\frac{3}{4}$ $\frac{5}{8}$ ◯ $\frac{5}{6}$

$\frac{2}{3}$ ◯ $\frac{2}{8}$ $\frac{4}{6}$ ◯ $\frac{4}{8}$

$\frac{3}{4}$ ◯ $\frac{3}{6}$ $\frac{2}{4}$ ◯ $\frac{2}{3}$

IXL.com
skill ID

PCW

Compare each pair of fractions. Fill in each circle with >, <, or =.

$\frac{1}{6}$ ◯ $\frac{1}{4}$ $\frac{1}{2}$ ◯ $\frac{1}{3}$

$\frac{2}{6}$ ◯ $\frac{3}{6}$ $\frac{3}{4}$ ◯ $\frac{1}{4}$

$\frac{4}{8}$ ◯ $\frac{4}{6}$ $\frac{2}{4}$ ◯ $\frac{2}{3}$

$\frac{2}{3}$ ◯ $\frac{1}{3}$ $\frac{2}{6}$ ◯ $\frac{2}{6}$

Challenge yourself! Write a fraction that makes each statement true.

$\frac{1}{4}$ < —— $\frac{2}{6}$ < ——

$\frac{5}{8}$ > —— $\frac{1}{2}$ > ——

IXL.com
skill ID
78D

Answer each question.

Milo and Jenna are reading the same book about Antarctica. Milo read $\frac{2}{6}$ of the book, and Jenna read $\frac{3}{6}$ of the book. Who read more?

_____

Ashley and Logan are both eating small pizzas for lunch. Ashley ate $\frac{5}{8}$ of her pizza, and Logan ate $\frac{4}{8}$ of his pizza. Who ate more?

_____

Carter and Jordan took their dogs for a walk. Carter walked $\frac{3}{4}$ of a mile, and Jordan walked $\frac{3}{8}$ of a mile. Who walked a longer distance?

_____

Riley and Claire are eating a loaf of banana bread from their grandmother. Riley ate $\frac{1}{6}$ of the loaf, and Logan ate $\frac{1}{8}$ of the loaf. Who ate more?

_____

Brandon and Audrey both bought large bags of popcorn for a movie. At the end of the movie, Brandon had $\frac{2}{4}$ of his popcorn left. Audrey had $\frac{1}{4}$ of her popcorn left. Who ate more?

_____

IXL.com
skill ID

9BK

Let's Learn!

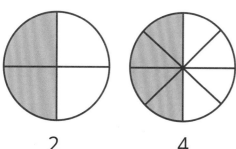

$$\frac{2}{4} = \frac{4}{8}$$

These models represent $\frac{2}{4}$ and $\frac{4}{8}$.

These two fractions are **equivalent**, or equal. The same amount of space is shaded in both.

Shade in the equivalent fraction. Write the new fraction.

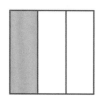
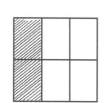

$$\frac{1}{3} \quad = \quad \frac{2}{6}$$

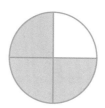

$$\frac{3}{4} \quad = \quad \underline{}$$

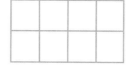

$$\frac{2}{4} \quad = \quad \underline{}$$

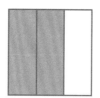

$$\frac{2}{3} \quad = \quad \underline{}$$

Shade in the equivalent fraction. Write the new fraction.

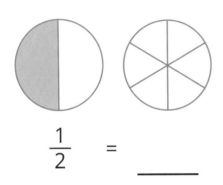

$$\frac{1}{4} = \underline{\quad\quad}$$

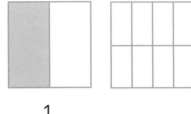

$$\frac{1}{2} = \underline{\quad\quad}$$

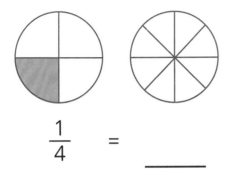

$$\frac{1}{2} = \underline{\quad\quad}$$

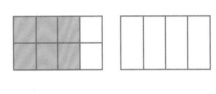

$$\frac{6}{8} = \underline{\quad\quad}$$

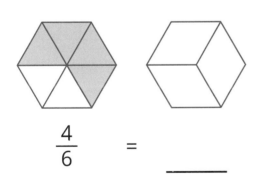

$$\frac{4}{6} = \underline{\quad\quad}$$

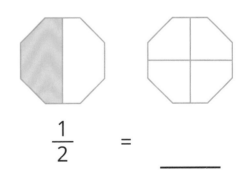

$$\frac{1}{2} = \underline{\quad\quad}$$

IXL.com
skill ID
ZJ2

Exploration Zone

ADDING FRACTIONS

You can use models to add fractions. Try it with $\frac{1}{6} + \frac{3}{6}$.

Start by shading $\frac{1}{6}$ of the rectangle. Then shade $\frac{3}{6}$ more of the rectangle.

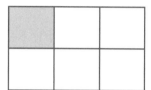 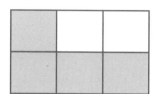

Now $\frac{4}{6}$ of the rectangle is shaded. So, $\frac{1}{6} + \frac{3}{6} = \frac{4}{6}$!

TRY IT YOURSELF!

Shade the models to find the sum.

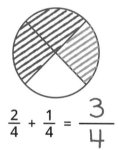

$\frac{2}{4} + \frac{1}{4} = \frac{3}{4}$

$\frac{5}{8} + \frac{2}{8} = $ ——

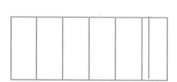

$\frac{1}{6} + \frac{2}{6} = $ ——

$\frac{1}{3} + \frac{1}{3} = $ ——

SUBTRACTING FRACTIONS

You can use models to subtract fractions, too. Try it with $\frac{5}{8} - \frac{2}{8}$.

Start by shading $\frac{5}{8}$ of the rectangle. Then take away $\frac{2}{8}$ of those shaded parts.

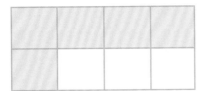 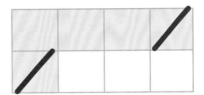

You have $\frac{3}{8}$ shaded parts left. So, $\frac{5}{8} - \frac{2}{8} = \frac{3}{8}$!

TRY IT YOURSELF!

Use the models to find the difference.

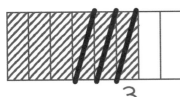

$$\frac{6}{8} - \frac{3}{8} = \frac{3}{8}$$

$$\frac{2}{3} - \frac{1}{3} = \underline{\hspace{1cm}}$$

$$\frac{4}{6} - \frac{1}{6} = \underline{\hspace{1cm}}$$

$$\frac{3}{4} - \frac{2}{4} = \underline{\hspace{1cm}}$$

How much money is there? Count the coins in each group.

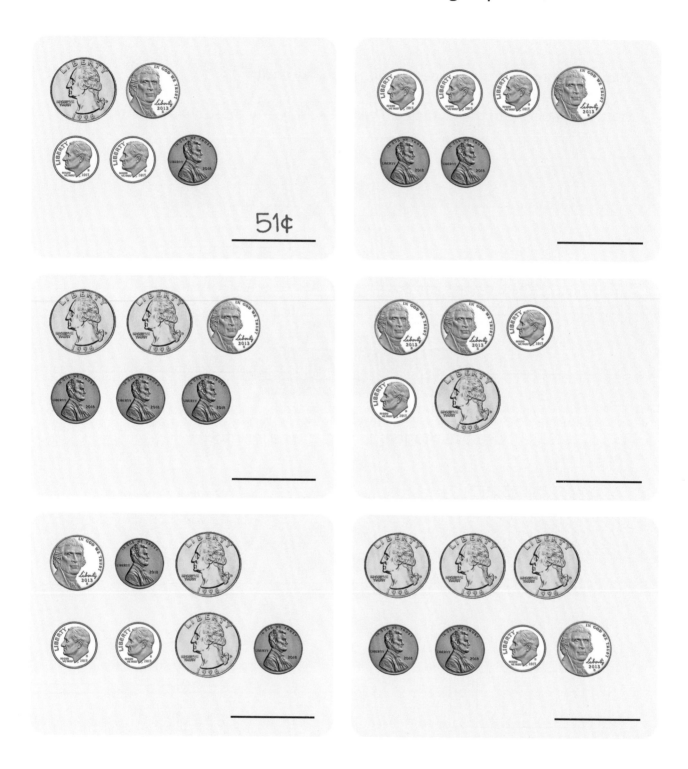

51¢

Count the money in each group.

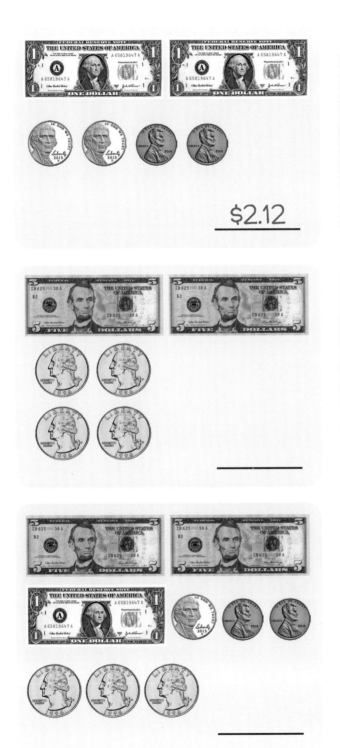

$2.12

_____

_____

_____

_____

IXL.com
skill ID
9RP

Answer each question.

Emily had $37. Her grandma gave her $25 for her birthday. How much money does Emily have now?

_____

Kaylee is at the museum gift shop. She wants to buy a package of astronaut ice cream for each of her 5 best friends. If each package of astronaut ice cream costs $7, how much money will Kaylee spend?

_____

Dylan has three $20 bills, and Matthew has a $100 bill. How much more money does Matthew have than Dylan?

_____

Oliver's grandfather has 8 five-dollar bills in his wallet. If he divides all of the bills evenly among his 4 grandchildren, how much money will each grandchild receive?

_____

Get ahead of the curve with extra math practice!

Scan this QR code for details.

Playground Palace has some items on sale. Use the poster to answer each question.

How much more does the play set cost than the playhouse?

_____

Sunrise Elementary School buys 5 seesaws. How much do the seesaws cost in all?

_____

The Creekside City Council bought 8 climbers for the city's parks. How much did the climbers cost in all?

_____

Mrs. Wilson buys the sandbox for half of the price shown on the poster. How much does she pay?

_____

IXL.com
skill ID
R6G

Let's Learn!

If you have money amounts like $5.20 or $4.40, you can still add or subtract. Line up the decimal points. Bring down the decimal point into the answer.

```
  $5. 2 0
+ $4. 4 0
---------
  $9. 6 0
```

```
  $6. 7 0
- $3. 3 0
---------
  $3. 4 0
```

Add or subtract.

```
  $1. 4 0
+ $3. 5 0
---------
```

```
  $8. 7 0
- $6. 3 0
---------
```

```
  $3. 2 5
+ $8. 0 3
---------
```

```
  $5. 8 5
- $2. 2 5
---------
```

```
  $4. 7 5
+ $3. 2 3
---------
```

```
  $6. 8 9
+ $5. 2 7
---------
```

```
  $8. 4 9
+ $1. 2 0
---------
```

```
  $6. 4 5
- $3. 1 0
---------
```

```
  $7. 3 1
- $2. 9 9
---------
```

```
  $7. 7 5
+ $4. 9 5
---------
```

```
  $8. 0 6
- $4. 3 9
---------
```

IXL.com
skill ID
AKZ

Answer each question.

Baker Farms: Market Stand

Apples
$3.00
per pound

Blueberries
$4.25
per basket

Tomatoes
$2.79
per basket

Flowers
$5.25
per bunch

Corn
4 for
$1.00

Potatoes
$1.39
per pound

Carrots
$2.60
per pound

Max bought a basket of blueberries and a pound of carrots. How much did he spend?

_____

How much more does a pound of carrots cost than a pound of potatoes?

_____

Kaitlyn bought 8 ears of corn and a basket of tomatoes. How much did she spent?

_____

Devon started with $20.00. He then bought one bunch of flowers and two pounds of apples. How much money does have left?

_____

IXL.com
skill ID
BK6

Let's Learn!

On a clock, the short hand points to the hour. The long hand points to the minute. For example, this clock shows 8:18.

The **short hand** on this clock is between 8 and 9. So, the hour is 8.

The **long hand** is at three marks after the number 3. It takes five minutes to get from one number to the next. So, the long hand shows 5 + 5 + 5 + 3 = 18 minutes past the hour.

Write the time.

__2:25__

_____

_____

_____

_____

_____

Draw the time.

7:15

5:45

11:27

3:52

10:30

8:58

IXL.com
skill ID
5ZQ

Grab a ruler. Measure the length of each object in inches.

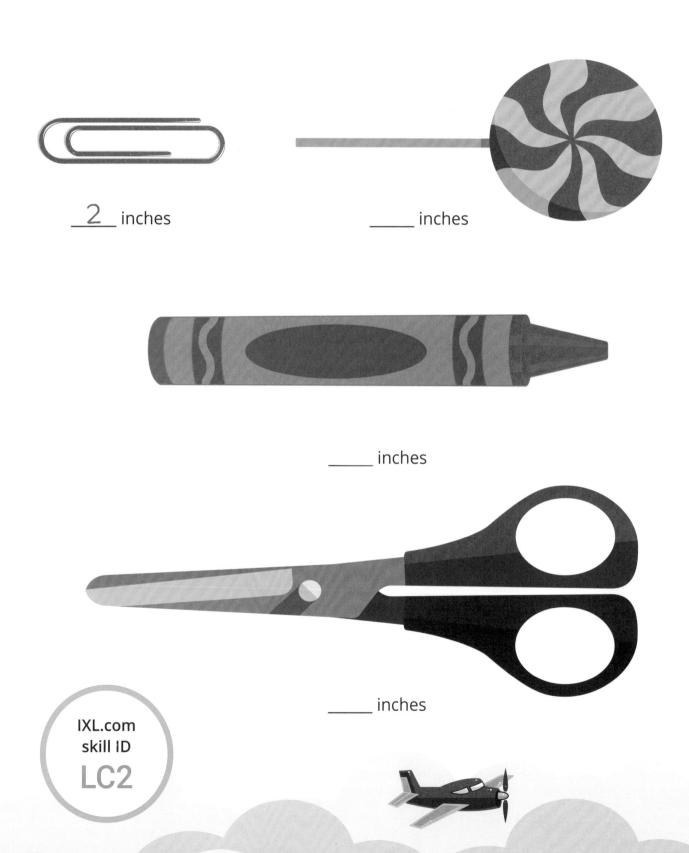

__2__ inches

_____ inches

_____ inches

_____ inches

IXL.com
skill ID
LC2

Measure the length of each object in centimeters.

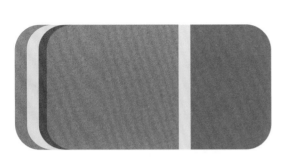

_____ centimeters

_____ centimeters

_____ centimeters

_____ centimeters

_____ centimeters

Let's Learn!

You can use **grams** or **kilograms** to measure an object's mass. Mass is similar to weight. A large paper clip has a mass of about 1 gram. A pineapple has a mass of about 1 kilogram, or 1,000 grams.

Circle the closest estimate.

(4 grams)   400 grams   4 kilograms

2 grams   200 grams   2 kilograms

9 grams   900 grams   9 kilograms

20 grams   200 grams   20 kilograms

IXL.com skill ID **FQ8**

For more practice, visit IXL.com or the IXL mobile app and enter this code in the search bar.

Let's Learn!

You can use **liters** or **milliliters** to measure an object's capacity, or how much the object can hold. There is 1 milliliter of milk in this teaspoon. This large water bottle holds 1 liter, or 1,000 milliliters, of water.

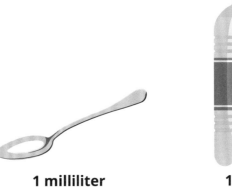

1 milliliter

1 liter

Circle the closest estimate.

(15 milliliters) 15 liters 150 liters

4 milliliters 4 liters 40 liters

300 milliliters 3 liters 300 liters

7 milliliters 700 milliliters 7 liters

Answer each question.

Rachel's doctor gave her 80 milliliters of medicine. She takes 8 milliliters of the medicine each day. How long will the medicine last?

_____ days

Aaliyah's dad started cooking dinner at 5:04 p.m. He was finished at 5:38 p.m. How long did it take Aaliyah's dad to cook dinner?

_____ minutes

Mrs. Wilson filled her baby's bathtub with 20 liters of water. It was too full, so she emptied some of the water. Now there are 17 liters of water in the bathtub. How much water did Mrs. Wilson empty out of the bathtub?

_____ liters

Cameron has a mass of 40 kilograms, which is 4 times the mass of his little brother. What is the mass of Cameron's brother?

_____ kilograms

IXL.com
skill ID
V9D

Answer each question.

Christian starting making brownies at 4:00 p.m. It took him 20 minutes to make the batter. He then baked the brownies in the oven for 28 minutes. At what time were the brownies finished?

_____

Makayla wants to drink 14 liters of water each week. How many liters of water should Makayla drink each day to reach her goal?

_____ liters

Sarah is making necklaces for her friends. She has 36 inches of string, and she wants each necklace to be 9 inches in length. How many necklaces can Sarah make?

_____ necklaces

Jordan's class has recess from 10:05 a.m. until 10:30 a.m. Their lunch break is 15 minutes longer than recess. How long is their lunch break?

_____ minutes

IXL.com
skill ID
VPW

Let's Learn!

A **polygon** is a flat shape with straight sides. Every polygon has a special name based on the number of sides it has!

| A **triangle** has 3 sides. | A **quadrilateral** has 4 sides. | A **pentagon** has 5 sides. | A **hexagon** has 6 sides. | An **octagon** has 8 sides. |

Write the name of each shape. Use the shape names above.

QUADRILATERAL

_____   _____

20% OFF **Dive into math practice with IXL!**

Get 20% off when you join IXL today.

Scan this QR code for details.

Keep going! Write the name of each shape. Use the names from page 188.

_____

_____

_____

_____

_____

_____

_____

_____

IXL.com
skill ID
JBT

Let's Learn!

There are many kinds of **quadrilaterals**. Here are a few of them.

A **parallelogram** has two pairs of parallel sides.

A **trapezoid** has one pair of parallel sides.

A **rectangle** is a parallelogram with four right angles.

A **rhombus** is a parallelogram with four equal side lengths.

A **square** is a parallelogram with four equal side lengths and four right angles. So, a square is also a rectangle and a rhombus.

Circle all of the quadrilaterals.

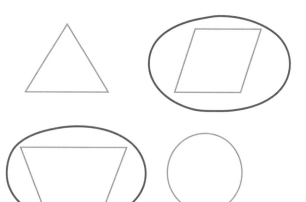

Circle all of the trapezoids.

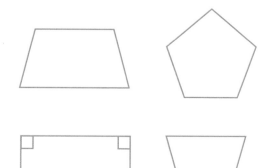

Circle all of the parallelograms.

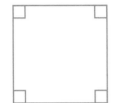 

Circle all of the squares.

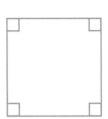 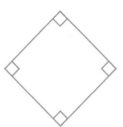

Circle all of the rhombuses.

 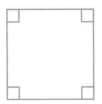

Circle all of the rectangles.

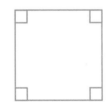 

IXL.com
skill ID
CNJ

Draw a rectangle that is not a square.

Draw a rhombus that is not a square.

Draw a quadrilateral that is not a trapezoid.

Draw a parallelogram that is not a rhombus.

Draw a quadrilateral that is not a parallelogram or a trapezoid.

Draw a rectangle that is also a rhombus. What is another name for this shape?

Draw at least 2 shapes in each part of the diagram.

Quadrilateral   Has a right angle

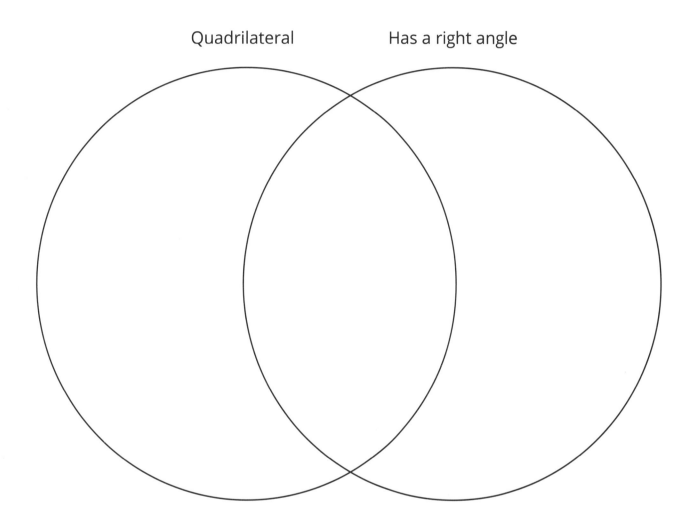

Boost your math learning
and save 20%!

Scan this QR code or visit
www.ixl.com/workbook/3u for details.

Let's Learn!

You buy a poster that is 4 feet long and 3 feet wide. What is its **area**? You can use multiplication to find out!

To find the area of a shape, break the shape into unit squares. Count or multiply to find the area.

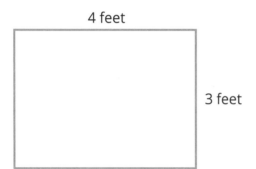

3 rows of 4 unit squares = 3 × 4 = 12 unit squares

In this problem, each unit square has an area of 1 square foot. So, the area of the poster is 12 square feet.

Split each shape into unit squares. Write the area.

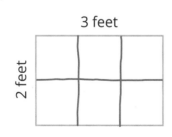

6 SQUARE FEET

5 feet

3 feet

_____

Find the area of each shape.

5 meters

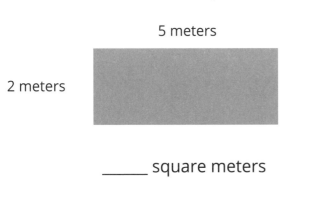

2 meters

_____ square meters

6 inches

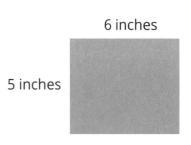

5 inches

_____ square inches

6 yards

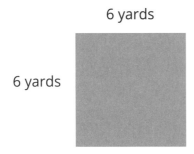

6 yards

_____ square yards

7 feet

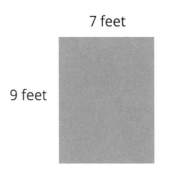

9 feet

_____ square feet

4 feet

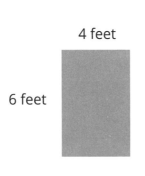

6 feet

_____ square feet

7 feet

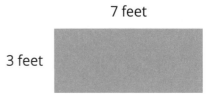

3 feet

_____ square feet

IXL.com
skill ID
8KJ

Write the missing side lengths.

5 INCHES

4 inches

Area = 20 square inches

4 meters

Area = 12 square meters

6 feet

Area = 42 square feet

3 yards

Area = 24 square yards

4 feet

Area = 28 square feet

9 feet

Area = 36 square feet

IXL.com
skill ID
X66

Let's Learn!

Can you find the area of this shape?

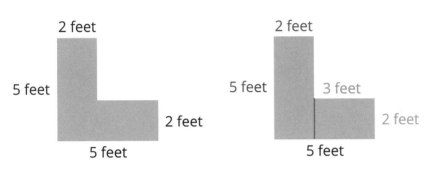

First, split it into two rectangles.

Then, subtract to find the missing side length.

Next, multiply to find the area of each rectangle, and then add to find the total area.

5 × 2 = 10 square feet   10 + 6 = 16 square feet

2 × 3 = 6 square feet

Find the area of each shape.

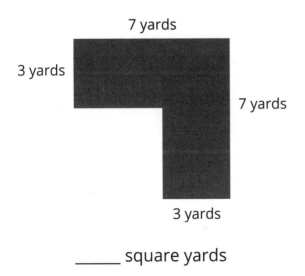

7 yards

3 yards

7 yards

3 yards

_____ square yards

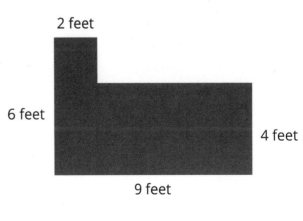

2 feet

6 feet

4 feet

9 feet

_____ square feet

Find the area of each shape.

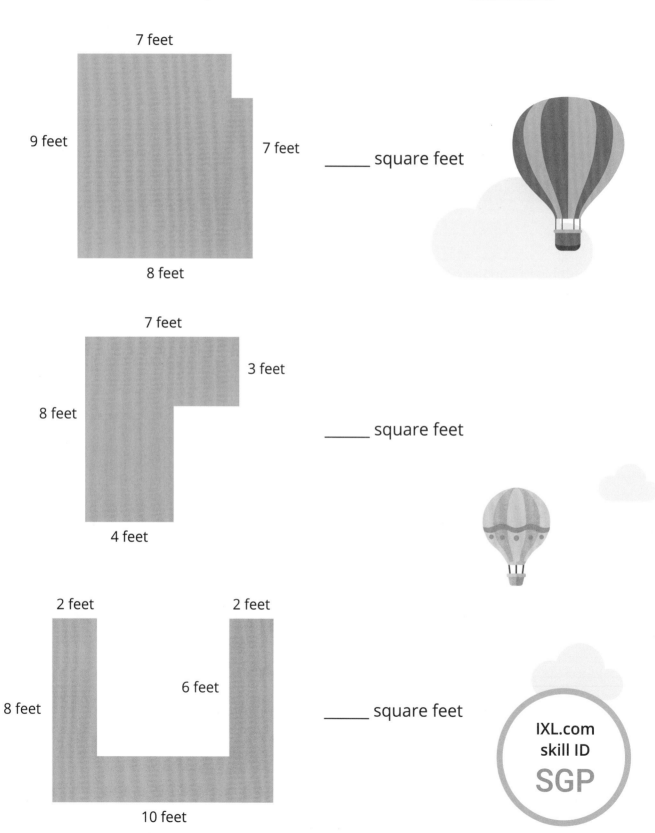

7 feet

9 feet   7 feet

8 feet

_____ square feet

7 feet

8 feet   3 feet

4 feet

_____ square feet

2 feet   2 feet

8 feet   6 feet

10 feet

_____ square feet

IXL.com
skill ID
SGP

The distance around a shape is its **perimeter**. You can add the lengths of all of the sides to find the perimeter. For example, the perimeter of this rectangle is 26 yards.

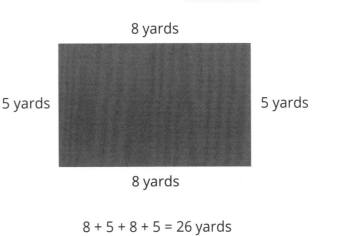

8 yards

5 yards   5 yards

8 yards

8 + 5 + 8 + 5 = 26 yards

Find the perimeter of each shape.

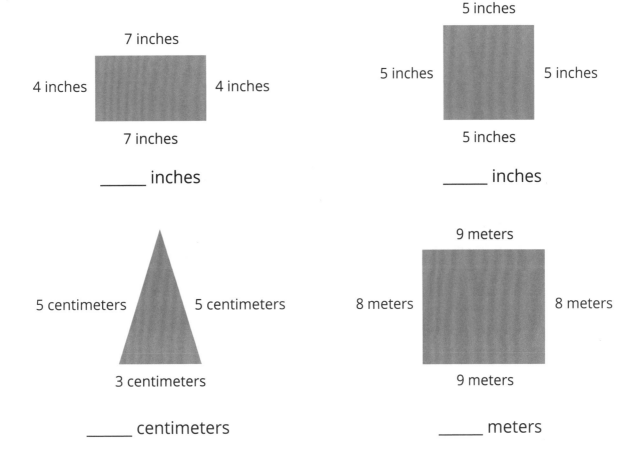

7 inches

4 inches   4 inches

7 inches

_____ inches

5 inches

5 inches   5 inches

5 inches

_____ inches

5 centimeters   5 centimeters

3 centimeters

_____ centimeters

9 meters

8 meters   8 meters

9 meters

_____ meters

Find the perimeter of each shape.

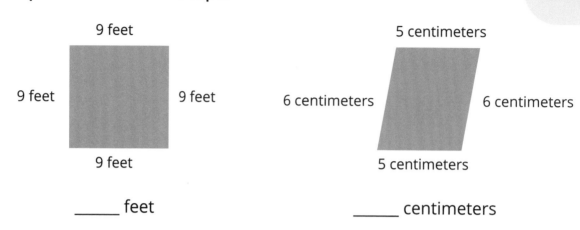

9 feet

9 feet   9 feet

9 feet

_____ feet

5 centimeters

6 centimeters   6 centimeters

5 centimeters

_____ centimeters

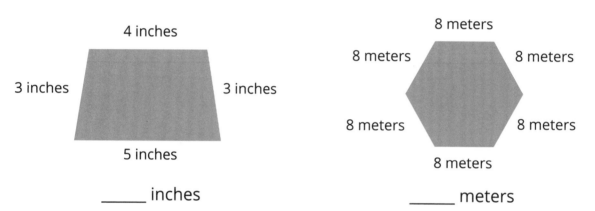

4 inches

3 inches   3 inches

5 inches

_____ inches

8 meters

8 meters   8 meters

8 meters   8 meters

8 meters

_____ meters

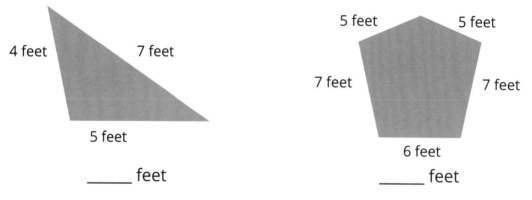

4 feet   7 feet

5 feet

_____ feet

5 feet   5 feet

7 feet   7 feet

6 feet

_____ feet

IXL.com
skill ID
LLY

Write the missing side lengths.

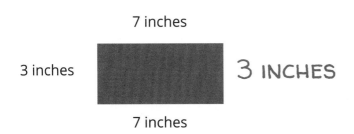

7 inches

3 inches   **3 INCHES**

7 inches

Perimeter = 20 inches

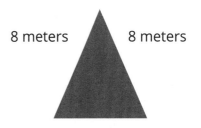

8 meters   8 meters

Perimeter = 22 meters

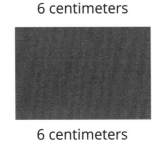

6 centimeters

6 centimeters

Perimeter = 20 centimeters

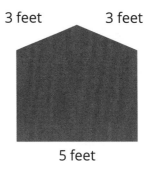

3 feet   3 feet

5 feet

Perimeter = 19 feet

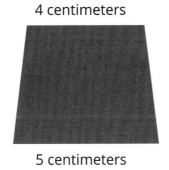

4 centimeters

5 centimeters

Perimeter = 19 centimeters

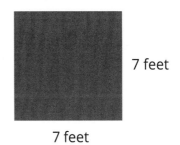

7 feet

7 feet

Perimeter = 28 feet

IXL.com
skill ID
T2V

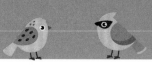

Use a ruler to measure the sides of each rectangle. Then find the area and the perimeter.

Perimeter = _____ inches   Area = _____ square inches

Perimeter = _____ inches   Area = _____ square inches

Answer each question.

The playground at Eastwood Park is shaped like a rectangle. It has a length of 9 yards and a width of 8 yards. What is the perimeter of the playground?

_____ yards

Lucy's bedroom is 9 feet long and 8 feet wide. What is the area of Lucy's bedroom floor?

_____ square feet

Julia has a quilt that is 6 feet long. It covers an area of 24 square feet. How wide is the quilt?

_____ feet

Leona has a rug in her bedroom that is shaped like a hexagon. All of the sides are the same length. If the perimeter of the rug is 18 feet, what is the length of each side?

_____ feet

Jack made a square poster for the Science Fair. The poster was 4 feet wide. What was the perimeter of the poster?

_____ feet

IXL.com
skill ID
CLD

Answer each question.

Jesse's family just moved into a new house with a big backyard. Jesse's dad bought a $785 play set for the yard. If it was on sale for $95 off, how much did Jesse's dad pay?

_____

Jesse's mom and dad want to put rubber padding underneath the play set. The padding is 6 meters long and 4 meters wide. What is the area of the padding?

_____ square meters

Jesse's mom wants to build a vegetable garden in their backyard. The garden will be shaped like a rectangle, and it will be 4 meters long and 2 meters wide. What will be the perimeter of the vegetable garden?

_____ meters

IXL.com
skill ID

CBA

Answer each question.

Jesse's mom has a pile of wooden planks. There are 22 meters of wood in all. If she puts wood around the perimeter of the garden, how many meters of wood will be left over?

_____ meters

Jesse's mom buys seeds to plant in the vegetable garden. Each packet of seeds cost $3. If Jesse's mom spends $27, how many seed packets does she buy?

_____ packets

Here is the layout of the area of the backyard. Draw places where the play set and garden could go.

Jesse's family wants to have grass on the area that is not covered by the play set or garden. What area of the backyard will have grass?

☐ = 1 square meter

_____ square meters

Each bag of grass seed will cover 3 square meters. How many bags of grass seed will the family need to buy?

_____ bags

The third graders at North Elementary School collected cans of food for a five-day drive. This chart shows how many cans were collected on each day.

	Monday	Tuesday	Wednesday	Thursday	Friday
Ms. Acosta's class	30	32	64	45	53
Mr. Maben's class	12	28	25	55	32
Ms. Fuller's class	35	32	42	50	36
Ms. Bailey's class	16	24	28	50	72

Answer each question.

What was the total number of cans collected on Monday?   _____ cans

How many cans did Mr. Maben's class collect in all?   _____ cans

On Wednesday, how many more cans did Ms. Fuller's class collect than Ms. Bailey's class?   _____ cans

Answer each question.

On Monday, Ms. Fuller's class packaged their cans into boxes. If each box could hold 7 cans, how many boxes did the class fill?

_____ boxes

On Friday, 12 students in Ms. Bailey's class brought in cans. Each student brought in the same number of cans. How many cans did each student bring?

_____ cans

Whose class collected the most cans overall?

_____

How many more cans did Ms. Fuller's class collect than Ms. Bailey's class?

_____ cans

One day, 11 students from the same class each brought in 5 cans of food. No one else from that class brought any cans that day. Whose class was this and on which day?

_____

IXL.com
skill ID
8FP

Allison's family is taking a four-day vacation to the beach. They have a total of $1,000 to spend on their trip. Answer each question.

It will cost Allison's family $30 to fill their gas tank each time they visit the gas station. They will stop at the gas station 3 times on the way to the beach. They will stop another 3 times on their way home. How much money will the family spend on gas?

_____

How much money is left, after gas?

_____

Allison's family will need to stay in a hotel for 4 nights. The cost of the hotel is $80 per night. How much money will they spend on the hotel?

_____

How much money is left, after gas and the hotel?

_____

Answer each question.

Allison and her brother will each get $20 for spending money, and their mom and dad will each get $50. How much money will be used for spending?

_____

The family will evenly divide the remaining money among the four days for food. How much money can they spend on food each day?

_____

If they eat 3 meals a day, how much money can they spend on each meal if the meals cost the same?

_____

On the last day of the trip, the family spent $16 on breakfast and $27 on lunch. How much money can they spend on dinner?

_____

IXL.com
skill ID

SRL

Answer key

PAGE 2
②6 ③4 5⑤0 ⑥1 3②5

2,①67 6,⓪99 ④37 8④2 2,②01

③,494 ⑤,721 50,998 6⑥72 7⑧,134

PAGE 3
97 ⟨397⟩ ⟨1,942⟩ 942

⟨276⟩ 76 999 ⟨1,000⟩

⟨635⟩ 563 ⟨2,643⟩ 2,346

768 ⟨867⟩ 687

390 329 ⟨392⟩

⟨5,372⟩ 5,237 5,273

PAGE 4
78 79 87

79 92 102

618 621 625

473 478 483 487

989 994 1,008 1,012

5,614 6,145 6,451 6,514

PAGE 5
500 1,400 800

4,900 2,500 1,000

25,000 5,000 3,000

6,000 7,000 15,000

41,000 29,000

88,000 60,000

PAGE 6
5 + 5 = 10   7 + 2 = 9

7 + 6 = 13   4 + 5 = 9

9 + 6 = 15   3 + 9 = 12

10 + 4 = 14   7 + 3 = 10

6 + 8 = 14   6 + 4 = 10

8 + 3 = 11   9 + 5 = 14

2 + 9 = 11   7 + 5 = 12

7 + 7 = 14   9 + 7 = 16

PAGE 7
4 + 7 = 11   5 + 8 = 13

10 + 6 = 16   10 + 10 = 20

8 + 9 = 17   9 + 4 = 13

3 + 8 = 11   6 + 9 = 15

9 + 10 = 19   5 + 6 = 11

6 + 7 = 13   5 + 9 = 14

8 + 8 = 16   7 + 8 = 15

4 + 8 = 12   8 + 6 = 14

10 + 7 = 17   9 + 9 = 18

PAGE 8
```
  56        39        27
+ 26      + 62      + 14
  82       101        41

  14        63        48
+ 45      + 87      + 76
  59       150       124
```

PAGE 9
```
  36        13        42
+ 38      + 75      + 66
  74        88       108

  58        40        39
+ 23      + 87      + 11
  81       127        50

  64        23        25
+ 82      + 57      + 48
 146        80        73

  56        94        77
+ 17      + 82      + 59
  73       176       136
```

When you add two even numbers or two odd numbers, you always get an even number. When you add an even number and an odd number, you always get an odd number.

PAGE 10
```
  53        49        77
  23        51        33
+ 63      + 87      + 23
 139       187       133

  23        98        43
  58        61        49
+ 87      + 56      + 14
 168       215       106

  34        61        73
  28        43        19
+ 50      + 39      + 82
 112       143       174

  86        70        94
  68        13        97
  82        46        75
+ 22      + 22      + 81
 258       151       347
```

PAGE 11
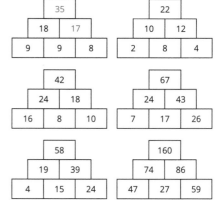

PAGE 12
```
  459       168       707
+ 256     + 365     + 285
  715       533       992

  383       448       754
+ 604     + 794     + 400
  987     1,242     1,154
```

PAGE 13
```
  375       285       812
+ 466     + 521     + 169
  841       806       981

  605       124       496
+ 326     + 747     + 275
  931       871       771

  148       299       758
+ 593     + 311     + 242
  741       610     1,000

  619       154       482
+ 309     + 768     + 249
  928       922       731
```

PAGE 14
```
  1,224     8,960     1,735
+ 1,008   + 1,363   + 4,778
  2,232    10,323     6,513

  3,672     4,800     2,236
+ 6,374   + 2,355   + 7,874
 10,046     7,155    10,110

  9,454     5,307     1,318
+ 4,828   + 6,624   + 8,097
 14,282    11,931     9,415

  8,524     7,475     5,629
+ 2,079   + 3,846   + 6,892
 10,603    11,321    12,521
```

PAGE 15

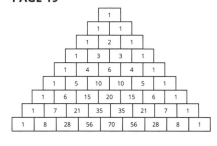

(Crossword grid)
1: 7
2: 2 8, 3: 1
1
4: 1 0 9, 5: 1
8, 2, 6: 9
1, 7: 7 3 4

PAGE 16

121 canoes

433 comic books

925 stickers

1,175 tickets

1,817 gallons

PAGE 17

209 seats

443 seats

652 seats

1,588 seats

PAGE 18

```
  144        836        555
  293        733        363
+ 416      + 487      + 179
  853      2,056      1,097

 7,411     8,675
 8,271     3,099
+2,455    +2,103
18,137    13,877

  234        655        513
  115        811        937
  641        632        614
+ 120      + 712      + 919
1,110      2,810      2,983

 4,714     9,339
 1,623     1,158
 5,950     9,702
+2,920    +5,851
15,207    26,050
```

PAGE 19

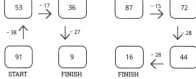

(Pascal's triangle)
```
                    1
                 1     1
              1     2     1
           1     3     3     1
        1     4     6     4     1
     1     5    10    10     5     1
  1     6    15    20    15     6     1
1  7   21    35    35    21     7     1
1  8  28   56   70   56   28    8    1
```

PAGE 20

11 − 5 = 6   17 − 8 = 9

12 − 3 = 9   13 − 9 = 4

15 − 8 = 7   12 − 8 = 4

12 − 5 = 7   16 − 7 = 9

11 − 9 = 2   15 − 9 = 6

10 − 7 = 3   13 − 5 = 8

13 − 8 = 5   11 − 7 = 4

14 − 6 = 8   14 − 5 = 9

11 − 2 = 9   13 − 7 = 6

15 − 6 = 9   11 − 8 = 3

PAGE 21

15 − 5 = 10   13 − 4 = 9   14 − 8 = 6

15 − 7 = 8   16 − 8 = 8   11 − 4 = 7

14 − 7 = 7   18 − 9 = 9   17 − 9 = 8

16 − 9 = 7   14 − 9 = 5   16 − 6 = 10

12 − 4 = 8   11 − 6 = 5   13 − 6 = 7

11 − 3 = 8   20 − 10 = 10   12 − 6 = 6

PAGE 22

```
  40        44        73
− 29      − 30      − 26
  11        14        47

  96        74        83
− 28      − 59      − 64
  68        15        19
```

PAGE 23

```
  94        84        70
− 56      − 48      − 54
  38        36        16

  37        94        41
− 11      − 14      − 22
  26        80        19

  54        62        83
− 15      − 13      − 55
  39        49        28

  60        89        91
− 48      − 78      − 27
  12        11        64

  83        84        72
− 42      − 35      − 68
  41        49         4
```

PAGE 24

```
  92        45        60
− 38      − 29      − 41
  54        16        19

  71        58        87
− 17      − 27      − 69
  54        31        18

  64        95        50
− 16      − 79      − 27
  48        16        23

  86        90        81
− 78      − 23      − 62
   8        67        19
```

PAGE 25

```
START      FINISH                  FINISH
 98         19          27  →−16→  11
−13↓      ↑−29        −29↑
 85  →−37→  48          56  ←−16←  72
                                  START

 53  →−17→  36          87  →−15→  72
                              START
−38↑      ↓−27                    ↓−28
 91         9          16  ←−28←  44
START     FINISH       FINISH
```

PAGE 26

```
  590        878        479
− 311      − 533      − 194
  279        345        285

  926        411        948
− 584      − 255      − 358
  342        156        590
```

PAGE 27

```
  754        960        922
− 652      − 467      − 619
  102        493        303

  782        510        733
− 694      − 374      − 163
   88        136        570

  934       (457)       762
− 312      −(392)     − 241
  622        (65)       521

  372        751        696
− 164      − 469      − 576
  208        282        120

  544        230       (574)
− 375      − 201      −(509)
  169         29        (65)
```

212 Answer key

PAGE 28

```
  905      701      802
- 427    - 165    - 385
  478      536      417

  779      602      525
- 477    - 439    - 471
  332      163       54

  518      945      702
- 113    - 695    - 310
  405      250      392

  805      831      300
- 723    - 599    - 174
   82      232      126
```

PAGE 29

```
  6,429     4,985     9,573
- 4,746   - 2,366   - 2,539
  1,683     2,619     7,034

  9,334     4,968     3,532
- 8,491   - 1,991   - 1,578
    843     2,977     1,954

  2,971     8,173     8,359
- 2,487   - 7,634   - 1,614
    484       539     6,745

  6,107     8,203     6,005
- 5,999   - 1,563   - 3,259
    108     6,640     2,746

  9,300     8,000     6,608
- 5,043   - 2,639   - 4,099
  4,257     5,361     2,509
```

PAGE 30

```
  6,980     6,861     8,856
- 3,882   - 3,763   - 7,878
  3,098     3,098       978

  9,549     7,385     2,583
- 1,863   - 4,287   - 1,605
  7,686     3,098       978

  3,132     3,103     5,155
- 1,805   - 1,922   - 4,177
  1,327     1,181       978
```

PAGE 31

```
  935      976      226
- 732    - 348    - 190
  203      628       36

  338      510      872
- 274    - 309    - 791
   64      201       81

  3,799     7,722     3,250
- 3,066   - 4,361   -   371
    733     3,361     2,879

  8,355     4,109     8,830
- 1,684   - 1,049   - 2,744
  6,671     3,060     6,086

  9,667     9,610
- 7,584   - 8,391
  2,083     1,219
```

PAGE 32

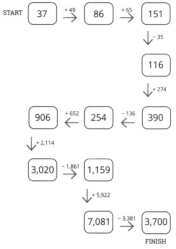

PAGE 33

87 tomatoes

$287

125 photos

179 lollipops

1,167 students

PAGE 34

```
   63        44        90
 - 17      + 93      - 67
   46       137        23

  253       171       284
+  29      -  38      +  19
  282       133       303

  712       750       758
+ 261      - 191      + 617
  973       559      1,375

  512       625       672
- 478      + 324      - 388
   34       949        284

  801       832       741
- 582      + 668      - 498
  219      1,500       243
```

PAGE 35

```
  8,023     6,540     1,819
+   933    +   276    -   403
  8,956     6,816     1,416

  9,957     9,292     5,138
- 1,024    + 3,423    - 3,349
  8,933    12,715     1,789

  4,687     3,021     4,351
+ 3,223    - 1,353    + 2,899
  7,910     1,668     7,250

  5,000     5,144     9,101
- 1,058    - 4,649    + 3,854
  3,942       495    12,955

  7,879     8,206     9,005
+ 5,414    - 2,949    - 4,497
 13,293     5,257     4,508
```

PAGE 36

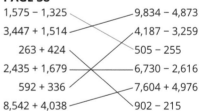

PAGE 37

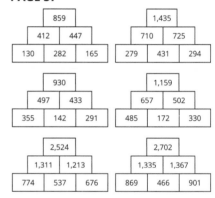

PAGE 38

1,575 − 1,325
3,447 + 1,514
263 + 424
2,435 + 1,679
592 + 336
8,542 + 4,038

9,834 − 4,873
4,187 − 3,259
505 − 255
6,730 − 2,616
7,604 + 4,976
902 − 215

PAGE 39

352 − 219 = 33 + 100

84 + 44 = 108 + 20

98 − 48 = 70 − 20

92 − 30 = 39 + 23

756 − 500 = 115 + 141

100 + 1,208 = 437 + 871

830 − 400 = 139 + 291

341 + 419 = 880 − 120

2,832 − 1,000 = 6,128 − 4,296

4,104 + 4,179 = 7,000 + 1,283

PAGE 40

134 ice pops

225 minutes

153 points

123 people

PAGE 41

4,221 miles

2,109 miles

2,112 miles

2,509 miles

PAGE 42

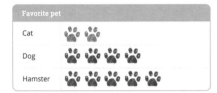

PAGE 43

30 muffins

25 muffins

90 muffins

160 muffins

PAGE 44

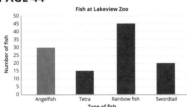

PAGE 45

15 days

10 days

10 days

90 days

PAGE 46

2 students

10 students

5 waves

2 waves

PAGE 47

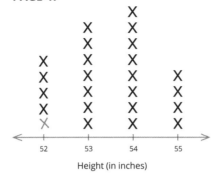

PAGE 48

3, 6, 9, 12, 15

2, 4, 6, 8, 10

5, 10, 15, 20, 25

10, 20, 30, 40, 50

PAGE 49

4 + 4 + 4 = 12
3 groups of 4 = 12
3 × 4 = 12

5 + 5 = 10
2 groups of 5 = 10
2 × 5 = 10

3 + 3 + 3 + 3 = 12
4 groups of 3 = 12
4 × 3 = 12

5 + 5 + 5 + 5 = 20
4 groups of 5 = 20
4 × 5 = 20

2 + 2 + 2 + 2 = 8
4 groups of 2 = 8
4 × 2 = 8

4 + 4 + 4 + 4 = 16
4 groups of 4 = 16
4 × 4 = 16

PAGE 50

2 + 2 + 2 + 2 + 2 = 10
5 groups of 2 = 10
5 × 2 = 10

3 + 3 + 3 + 3 + 3 = 15
5 groups of 3 = 15
5 × 3 = 15

4 + 4 + 4 + 4 + 4 = 20
5 groups of 4 = 20
5 × 4 = 20

PAGE 51

2 rows of 4 = 8   3 rows of 3 = 9
2 × 4 = 8   3 × 3 = 9

4 rows of 3 = 12   3 rows of 2 = 6
4 × 3 = 12   3 × 2 = 6

2 rows of 5 = 10
2 × 5 = 10

PAGE 52

2 rows of 4 = 8   3 rows of 4 = 12
2 × 4 = 8   3 × 4 = 12

3 rows of 6 = 18   4 rows of 4 = 16
3 × 6 = 18   4 × 4 = 16

PAGE 53

The product is 20. The factors are 5 and 4.

2 × 3 = 6   The product is 6.

2 × 5 = 10   The other factor is 5.

4 × 4 = 16

PAGE 54

2 × 4 = 8   2 × 8 = 16
3 × 4 = 12   2 × 5 = 10
2 × 2 = 4   2 × 9 = 18
3 × 8 = 24   2 × 10 = 20
2 × 3 = 6   3 × 6 = 18
3 × 3 = 9   2 × 6 = 12
3 × 1 = 3   2 × 7 = 14
3 × 7 = 21   3 × 2 = 6
3 × 9 = 27   3 × 5 = 15

All the multiples of 2 are even numbers.

PAGE 55

2 × 6 = 12   3 × 8 = 24   3 × 2 = 6
2 × 8 = 16   2 × 2 = 4   2 × 9 = 18
3 × 10 = 30   3 × 5 = 15   3 × 9 = 27
2 × 7 = 14   3 × 1 = 3   2 × 3 = 6
2 × 4 = 8   3 × 6 = 18   2 × 1 = 2
3 × 3 = 9   3 × 7 = 21   3 × 4 = 12

PAGE 56

5 × 3 = 15	5 × 7 = 35
4 × 1 = 4	4 × 6 = 24
4 × 2 = 8	5 × 2 = 10
5 × 4 = 20	4 × 9 = 36
4 × 7 = 28	4 × 8 = 32
4 × 10 = 40	5 × 9 = 45
5 × 1 = 5	5 × 8 = 40
4 × 5 = 20	4 × 3 = 12
5 × 10 = 50	4 × 4 = 16
5 × 6 = 30	5 × 5 = 25

The last digit of each multiple of 5 is either 5 or 0.

PAGE 57

4 × 10 = 40	4 × 6 = 24	4 × 3 = 12
5 × 5 = 25	5 × 8 = 40	4 × 9 = 36
5 × 7 = 35	4 × 8 = 32	5 × 1 = 5
4 × 4 = 16	5 × 10 = 50	5 × 6 = 30
4 × 7 = 28	4 × 1 = 4	4 × 5 = 20
5 × 3 = 15	5 × 4 = 20	5 × 9 = 45

PAGE 58

5 × 4 = 20	2 × 7 = 14
3 × 8 = 24	5 × 8 = 40
2 × 9 = 18	3 × 3 = 9
4 × 8 = 32	2 × 5 = 10
3 × 6 = 18	4 × 10 = 40
5 × 7 = 35	3 × 2 = 6
4 × 9 = 36	5 × 5 = 25
2 × 1 = 2	4 × 4 = 16
3 × 4 = 12	5 × 10 = 50
5 × 6 = 30	2 × 8 = 16

PAGE 59

4 × 2 = 8	3 × 7 = 21
5 × 1 = 5	3 × 5 = 15
2 × 6 = 12	4 × 3 = 12
4 × 5 = 20	3 × 1 = 3
2 × 10 = 20	4 × 6 = 24
5 × 2 = 10	5 × 9 = 45
2 × 2 = 4	3 × 9 = 27
5 × 3 = 15	3 × 10 = 30
2 × 4 = 8	4 × 7 = 28

PAGE 60

2 × 6 = 12	3 × 5 = 15
3 × 8 = 24	4 × 7 = 28
2 × 7 = 14	2 × 9 = 18
5 × 4 = 20	5 × 6 = 30
4 × 8 = 32	4 × 9 = 36
5 × 9 = 45	5 × 8 = 40

PAGE 61

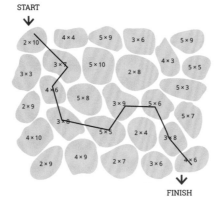

START

FINISH

PAGE 62

10 pounds

24 students

15 granola bars

14 googly eyes

18 sandwiches

PAGE 63

21 apples

12 oranges

10 bananas

50 cents

PAGE 64

5 × 3 = 15	5 × 8 = 40
3 × 5 = 15	8 × 5 = 40
4 × 7 = 28	2 × 9 = 18
7 × 4 = 28	9 × 2 = 18
3 × 7 = 21	5 × 10 = 50
7 × 3 = 21	10 × 5 = 50
4 × 9 = 36	3 × 6 = 18
9 × 4 = 36	6 × 3 = 18

The products are the same in each pair.

PAGE 65

6 × 3 = 18	6 × 5 = 30
7 × 10 = 70	7 × 9 = 63
7 × 8 = 56	6 × 2 = 12
7 × 4 = 28	7 × 6 = 42
6 × 1 = 6	7 × 3 = 21
7 × 5 = 35	6 × 6 = 36
6 × 10 = 60	6 × 4 = 24
7 × 7 = 49	7 × 1 = 7
6 × 8 = 48	6 × 7 = 42
7 × 2 = 14	6 × 9 = 54

PAGE 66

8 × 2 = 16	9 × 5 = 45
9 × 7 = 63	9 × 4 = 36
8 × 9 = 72	8 × 6 = 48
8 × 1 = 8	9 × 2 = 18
9 × 3 = 27	9 × 8 = 72
8 × 5 = 40	9 × 1 = 9
8 × 8 = 64	8 × 10 = 80
9 × 6 = 54	9 × 9 = 81
8 × 4 = 32	8 × 3 = 24
9 × 10 = 90	8 × 7 = 56

The digits have a sum of 9.

PAGE 67

7 × 2 = 14	9 × 9 = 81	6 × 3 = 18
6 × 1 = 6	7 × 6 = 42	8 × 10 = 80
8 × 2 = 16	8 × 4 = 32	6 × 9 = 54
7 × 7 = 49	9 × 8 = 72	6 × 5 = 30
8 × 3 = 24	6 × 10 = 60	9 × 10 = 90
9 × 4 = 36	7 × 9 = 63	7 × 8 = 56
6 × 6 = 36	7 × 4 = 28	8 × 8 = 64

PAGE 68

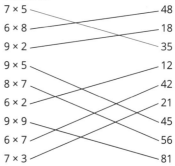

7 × 5	48
6 × 8	18
9 × 2	35
9 × 5	12
8 × 7	42
6 × 2	21
9 × 9	45
6 × 7	56
7 × 3	81

PAGE 69

7 × 8 = 56	6 × 4 = 24
8 × 6 = 48	8 × 5 = 40
8 × 8 = 64	7 × 4 = 28
9 × 6 = 54	7 × 10 = 70
6 × 5 = 30	9 × 3 = 27
9 × 4 = 36	7 × 7 = 49
6 × 7 = 42	6 × 2 = 12
7 × 3 = 21	9 × 1 = 9
9 × 7 = 63	9 × 9 = 81

PAGE 70

35 cinnamon rolls

56 marshmallows

48 stickers

54 people

PAGE 71

18 blocks

$32

60 pieces of sushi

No. He will have read only 40 pages.

PAGE 72

3 × 10 = 30	10 × 5 = 50
10 × 7 = 70	1 × 10 = 10
6 × 10 = 60	10 × 10 = 100
10 × 2 = 20	4 × 10 = 40
8 × 10 = 80	10 × 9 = 90
10 × 3 = 30	10 × 6 = 60
5 × 10 = 50	10 × 8 = 80
9 × 10 = 90	2 × 10 = 20
10 × 4 = 40	7 × 10 = 70

PAGE 73

7 × 10 = 70	10 × 2 = 20	10 × 6 = 60
10 × 1 = 10	5 × 10 = 50	10 × 10 = 100
9 × 10 = 90	10 × 3 = 30	7 × 10 = 70
6 × 10 = 60	10 × 8 = 80	10 × 2 = 20
10 × 10 = 100	4 × 10 = 40	10 × 5 = 50

PAGE 74

2 × 40 = 80	6 × 20 = 120	7 × 30 = 210
3 × 30 = 90	5 × 70 = 350	4 × 30 = 120
9 × 20 = 180	3 × 80 = 240	5 × 40 = 200
6 × 50 = 300	7 × 70 = 490	4 × 80 = 320

PAGE 75

5 × 300 = 1,500

4 × 600 = 2,400

3 × 900 = 2,700

2 × 800 = 1,600

6 × 700 = 4,200

7 × 200 = 1,400

8 × 700 = 5,600

9 × 400 = 3,600

6 × 800 = 4,800

5 × 400 = 2,000

8 × 800 = 6,400

5 × 600 = 3,000

PAGE 76

3 × 6,000 = 18,000

3 × 60,000 = 180,000

3 × 600,000 = 1,800,000

5 × 7,000 = 35,000

8 × 40,000 = 320,000

4 × 50,000 = 200,000

3 × 90,000 = 270,000

9 × 200,000 = 1,800,000

4 × 3,000,000 = 12,000,000

9 × 9,000,000 = 81,000,000

5 × 6,000,000 = 30,000,000

PAGE 77

24,000 pounds

280,000 packs

1,000 days

PAGE 78

6 × 4 = 24	6 × 8 = 48
5 × 5 = 25	4 × 3 = 12
10 × 8 = 80	3 × 9 = 27
3 × 5 = 15	2 × 10 = 20
2 × 7 = 14	9 × 8 = 72
8 × 2 = 16	8 × 4 = 32
7 × 3 = 21	9 × 5 = 45
7 × 6 = 42	10 × 4 = 40
6 × 5 = 30	7 × 5 = 35
8 × 8 = 64	9 × 10 = 90

PAGE 79

6 × 3 = 18	3 × 8 = 24	2 × 3 = 6
4 × 2 = 8	3 × 4 = 12	3 × 10 = 30
5 × 4 = 20	6 × 6 = 36	9 × 3 = 27
2 × 8 = 16	8 × 5 = 40	4 × 7 = 28
7 × 10 = 70	7 × 7 = 49	8 × 6 = 48
9 × 6 = 54	3 × 7 = 21	4 × 9 = 36
7 × 9 = 63	5 × 6 = 30	7 × 8 = 56

PAGE 80

4

9

15

7

5

7

PAGE 81

Age	Ruby	Micah	Sarah	Charlie	Zach
5	x				
10					x
15			x		
20		x			
40			x		

PAGE 82

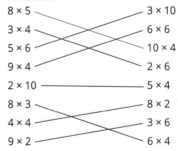

PAGE 83

4 × 4 = 16

5 × 5 = 25	6 × 6 = 36	7 × 7 = 49
8 × 8 = 64	9 × 9 = 81	10 × 10 = 100

Answer key

PAGE 84

0 × 3 = 0	1 × 4 = 4
10 × 0 = 0	1 × 2 = 2
5 × 1 = 5	0 × 7 = 0
1 × 0 = 0	10 × 1 = 10
8 × 0 = 0	1 × 8 = 8
1 × 6 = 6	0 × 6 = 0
0 × 9 = 0	1 × 1 = 1
3 × 1 = 3	2 × 0 = 0
9 × 1 = 9	0 × 5 = 0
4 × 0 = 0	1 × 7 = 7

When you multiply by 0, you always get 0 as the answer. When you multiply 1 by any number, the answer is always that number.

PAGE 85

25 × 1 = 25	79 × 0 = 0
0 × 98 = 0	1 × 528 = 528
0 × 654 = 0	377 × 0 = 0
0 × 710 = 0	498 × 1 = 498
1 × 5,122 = 5,122	6,936 × 0 = 0
2,628 × 1 = 2,628	0 × 4,876 = 0
1 × 7,301 = 7,301	9,620 × 1 = 9,620
0 × 5,644 = 0	1 × 9,979 = 9,979

PAGE 86

11 × 3 = 33	12 × 8 = 96
12 × 4 = 48	11 × 8 = 88
12 × 5 = 60	11 × 5 = 55
11 × 2 = 22	11 × 9 = 99
12 × 2 = 24	11 × 12 = 132
11 × 7 = 77	12 × 12 = 144
11 × 10 = 110	12 × 7 = 84
12 × 10 = 120	11 × 4 = 44
12 × 3 = 36	12 × 6 = 72
11 × 6 = 66	12 × 9 = 108

PAGE 87

12 × 5 = 60	11 × 7 = 77
12 × 3 = 36	11 × 11 = 121
12 × 4 = 48	11 × 4 = 44
12 × 8 = 96	12 × 7 = 84
11 × 8 = 88	11 × 12 = 132
12 × 6 = 72	12 × 9 = 108
12 × 10 = 120	11 × 11 = 121
12 × 2 = 24	11 × 10 = 110
11 × 9 = 99	12 × 11 = 132

PAGE 88

(8 × 9 = 72)	12 × 3 = 36	1 × 10 = 10
4 × 7 = 28	11 × 2 = 22	(8 × 12 = 96)
5 × 12 = 60	4 × 8 = 32	5 × 11 = 55
12 × 1 = 12	(9 × 9 = 81)	5 × 4 = 20
6 × 7 = 42	7 × 8 = 56	8 × 6 = 48
7 × 3 = 21	7 × 10 = 70	4 × 12 = 48
5 × 6 = 30	8 × 8 = 64	9 × 4 = 36
3 × 8 = 24	6 × 6 = 36	12 × 0 = 0

PAGE 89

8 × 2 = 16	(5 × 0 = 0)	4 × 10 = 40
5 × 5 = 25	9 × 3 = 27	12 × 5 = 60
10 × 12 = 120	(1 × 11 = 11)	7 × 9 = 63
2 × 9 = 18	7 × 7 = 49	3 × 5 = 15
10 × 10 = 100	12 × 9 = 108	5 × 4 = 20
(3 × 3 = 9)	11 × 12 = 132	2 × 6 = 12
9 × 6 = 54	4 × 4 = 16	8 × 12 = 96
5 × 9 = 45	2 × 10 = 20	7 × 11 = 77

PAGE 90

9 × 7 = 63	10 × 6 = 60
12 × 5 = 60	1 × 5 = 5
0 × 12 = 0	3 × 6 = 18
6 × 7 = 42	8 × 4 = 32
	6 × 8 = 48
	4 × 12 = 48

PAGE 91

24 sweet potatoes

72 bagels

81 chairs

28 quarters

88 players

PAGE 92

(3 × 2) × 4 = 6 × 4 = 24
3 × (2 × 4) = 3 × 8 = 24

(5 × 2) × 3 = 10 × 3 = 30
5 × (2 × 3) = 5 × 6 = 30

(2 × 2) × 4 = 4 × 4 = 16
2 × (2 × 4) = 2 × 8 = 16

PAGE 93

Answers may vary for the first two problems. Some possible answers are shown below.

(2 × 2) × 1 × 3 = 4 × (1 × 3) = 4 × 3 = 12

2 × 2 × (1 × 3) = 2 × (2 × 3) = 2 × 6 = 12

2 × (2 × 1) × 3 = (2 × 2) × 3 = 4 × 3 = 12

(3 × 2) × 4 × 2 = 6 × (4 × 2) = 6 × 8 = 48

3 × 2 × (4 × 2) = (3 × 2) × 8 = 6 × 8 = 48

3 × (2 × 4) × 2 = (3 × 8) × 2 = 24 × 2 = 48

3 × 3 × 2 = 18

4 × 2 × 4 = 32

4 × 3 × 3 = 36

PAGE 94

6 × 12 = 6 × (10 + 2)

6 × 12 = (6 × 10) + (6 × 2)

6 × 12 = 60 + 12

6 × 12 = 72

7 × 16 = 7 × (10 + 6)

7 × 16 = (7 × 10) + (7 × 6)

7 × 16 = 70 + 42

7 × 16 = 112

PAGE 95

4 × 17 = 4 × (10 + 7)

4 × 17 = (4 × 10) + (4 × 7)

4 × 17 = 40 + 28

4 × 17 = 68

8 × 23 = 8 × (20 + 3)

8 × 23 = (8 × 20) + (8 × 3)

8 × 23 = 160 + 24

8 × 23 = 184

9 × 45 = 9 × (40 + 5)

9 × 45 = (9 × 40) + (9 × 5)

9 × 45 = 360 + 45

9 × 45 = 405

PAGE 96

53 × 2 —— 1 0 6	84 × 2 —— 1 6 8	92 × 3 —— 2 7 6
72 × 4 —— 2 8 8	31 × 8 —— 2 4 8	41 × 5 —— 2 0 5

PAGE 97

32 × 3 = 96	43 × 2 = 86	92 × 4 = 368
83 × 3 = 249	61 × 7 = 427	51 × 8 = 408
42 × 4 = 168	72 × 3 = 216	91 × 5 = 455
61 × 8 = 488	60 × 3 = 180	82 × 4 = 328

PAGE 98

58 × 5 = 290	83 × 7 = 581	44 × 8 = 352
29 × 4 = 116	97 × 6 = 582	82 × 8 = 656

PAGE 99

59 × 2 = 118	64 × 8 = 512	44 × 5 = 220
35 × 3 = 105	42 × 5 = 210	73 × 6 = 438
93 × 6 = 558	84 × 4 = 336	49 × 9 = 441
94 × 8 = 752	87 × 5 = 435	97 × 8 = 776
58 × 8 = 464	39 × 3 = 117	75 × 8 = 600

PAGE 100

62 × 7 = 434	23 × 4 = 92	18 × 9 = 162
56 × 2 = 112	54 × 6 = 324	31 × 9 = 279
83 × 3 = 249	67 × 4 = 268	35 × 5 = 175
28 × 6 = 168	29 × 7 = 203	86 × 6 = 516
35 × 6 = 210	45 × 9 = 405	47 × 7 = 329

PAGE 101

128 cups

$100

144 mini muffins

144 third graders

512 grams

PAGE 102

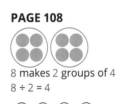

3^4 — $3 \times 3 \times 3 \times 3$

2^3 — $2 \times 2 \times 2$

4^2 — 4×4

5^2 — 5×5

5^4 — $5 \times 5 \times 5 \times 5$

PAGE 103

$6^3 = 6 \times 6 \times 6 = 216$

$9^2 = 9 \times 9 = 81$

$2^5 = 2 \times 2 \times 2 \times 2 \times 2 = 32$

$5^3 = 5 \times 5 \times 5 = 125$

$3^4 = 3 \times 3 \times 3 \times 3 = 81$

$8^2 = 8 \times 8 = 64$

$4^4 = 4 \times 4 \times 4 \times 4 = 256$

$7^3 = 7 \times 7 \times 7 = 343$

Exponents with 10			
10^2	100	2 zeros	hundred
10^3	1,000	3 zeros	thousand
10^4	10,000	4 zeros	ten thousand
10^6	1,000,000	6 zeros	million
10^9	1,000,000,000	9 zeros	billion
10^{12}	1,000,000,000,000	12 zeros	trillion

PAGE 104

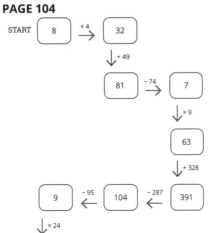

START 8 →×4 32 →+49 81 →−74 7 →×9 63 →+328 391 →−287 104 →−95 9 →×24 216 →+1,358 1,574 FINISH

PAGE 105

63 × 4 = 252	53 − 28 = 25	45 + 67 = 112
640 − 164 = 476	85 × 7 = 595	379 + 339 = 718
426 + 325 = 751	605 − 124 = 481	84 × 8 = 672
4,221 + 1,885 = 6,106	5,320 − 2,866 = 2,454	8,442 − 7,851 = 591
3,556 + 6,449 = 10,005	92 × 6 = 552	78 × 5 = 390

PAGE 106

26 cereal bars

47 animals

$527

429 scoops

$2

PAGE 107

292 beads

893 miles

5 times

61 pages

PAGE 108

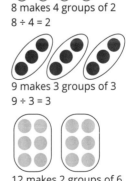

8 makes 2 groups of 4
8 ÷ 2 = 4

8 makes 4 groups of 2
8 ÷ 4 = 2

9 makes 3 groups of 3
9 ÷ 3 = 3

12 makes 2 groups of 6
12 ÷ 2 = 6

Answer key

PAGE 108, continued

15 makes 5 groups of 3
15 ÷ 5 = 3

20 makes 4 groups of 5
20 ÷ 4 = 5

PAGE 109

6 ÷ 3 = 2

6 ÷ 2 = 3

15 ÷ 5 = 3

16 ÷ 4 = 4

PAGE 110

2 × 4 = 8
8 ÷ 2 = 4

3 × 3 = 9
9 ÷ 3 = 3

3 × 5 = 15
15 ÷ 3 = 5

5 × 4 = 20
20 ÷ 5 = 4

PAGE 111

2 × 5 = 10

12 ÷ 3 = 4

6 ÷ 3 = 2

4 × 2 = 8

5 × 5 = 25

16 ÷ 4 = 4

PAGE 112

Fact family arrangements may vary.

2 × 4 = 8	5 × 4 = 20
4 × 2 = 8	4 × 5 = 20
8 ÷ 2 = 4	20 ÷ 5 = 4
8 ÷ 4 = 2	20 ÷ 4 = 5
3 × 5 = 15	4 × 3 = 12
5 × 3 = 15	3 × 4 = 12
15 ÷ 5 = 3	12 ÷ 3 = 4
15 ÷ 3 = 5	12 ÷ 4 = 3

PAGE 113

Fact family arrangements may vary.

3 × 7 = 21	2 × 8 = 16
7 × 3 = 21	8 × 2 = 16
21 ÷ 7 = 3	16 ÷ 8 = 2
21 ÷ 3 = 7	16 ÷ 2 = 8
6 × 2 = 12	3 × 6 = 18
2 × 6 = 12	6 × 3 = 18
12 ÷ 2 = 6	18 ÷ 3 = 6
12 ÷ 6 = 2	18 ÷ 6 = 3
6 × 4 = 24	
4 × 6 = 24	
24 ÷ 4 = 6	
24 ÷ 6 = 4	

PAGE 114

14 ÷ 2 = 7	6 ÷ 3 = 2	2 ÷ 2 = 1
12 ÷ 3 = 4	18 ÷ 3 = 6	21 ÷ 3 = 7
6 ÷ 2 = 3	3 ÷ 3 = 1	8 ÷ 2 = 4
27 ÷ 3 = 9	12 ÷ 2 = 6	9 ÷ 3 = 3
4 ÷ 2 = 2	16 ÷ 2 = 8	30 ÷ 3 = 10
20 ÷ 2 = 10	15 ÷ 3 = 5	10 ÷ 2 = 5

PAGE 115

20 ÷ 4 = 5	15 ÷ 5 = 3	36 ÷ 4 = 9
35 ÷ 5 = 7	16 ÷ 4 = 4	4 ÷ 4 = 1
50 ÷ 5 = 10	45 ÷ 5 = 9	30 ÷ 5 = 6
8 ÷ 4 = 2	10 ÷ 5 = 2	24 ÷ 4 = 6
20 ÷ 5 = 4	40 ÷ 5 = 8	12 ÷ 4 = 3
32 ÷ 4 = 8	25 ÷ 5 = 5	40 ÷ 4 = 10

PAGE 116

9 ÷ 3 = 3	20 ÷ 5 = 4
12 ÷ 4 = 3	10 ÷ 2 = 5
50 ÷ 5 = 10	20 ÷ 4 = 5
20 ÷ 2 = 10	15 ÷ 3 = 5
6 ÷ 2 = 3	10 ÷ 5 = 2
24 ÷ 3 = 8	28 ÷ 4 = 7
36 ÷ 4 = 9	12 ÷ 2 = 6
35 ÷ 5 = 7	21 ÷ 3 = 7
16 ÷ 4 = 4	16 ÷ 2 = 8
27 ÷ 3 = 9	45 ÷ 5 = 9

PAGE 117

16 ÷ 4 = 4	18 ÷ 3 = 6	5 ÷ 5 = 1
14 ÷ 2 = 7	8 ÷ 4 = 2	12 ÷ 3 = 4
25 ÷ 5 = 5	24 ÷ 4 = 6	40 ÷ 4 = 10
8 ÷ 2 = 4	30 ÷ 5 = 6	18 ÷ 2 = 9
32 ÷ 4 = 8	15 ÷ 5 = 3	30 ÷ 3 = 10
40 ÷ 5 = 8	6 ÷ 3 = 2	28 ÷ 4 = 7

PAGE 118

24 ÷ 3   40 ÷ 4
28 ÷ 4   27 ÷ 3
50 ÷ 5   16 ÷ 2
45 ÷ 5   21 ÷ 3
8 ÷ 2   16 ÷ 4
15 ÷ 5   18 ÷ 3
30 ÷ 5   9 ÷ 3

PAGE 119

25 ÷ 5 = 5	12 ÷ 3 = 4
16 ÷ 4 = 4	15 ÷ 5 = 3
21 ÷ 3 = 7	4 ÷ 2 = 2
28 ÷ 4 = 7	35 ÷ 5 = 7
12 ÷ 2 = 6	3 ÷ 3 = 1
20 ÷ 5 = 4	18 ÷ 3 = 6
40 ÷ 4 = 10	24 ÷ 4 = 6
24 ÷ 3 = 8	14 ÷ 2 = 7

PAGE 120

8 plates of pasta

6 cans

4 roses

10 small bags

9 fish

PAGE 121

6 sticky hands

5 whistles

7 jars of bubbles

4 slap bracelets

PAGE 122

The dividend is 21. The divisor is 3. The quotient is 7.

$20 \div 4 = 5$ The dividend is 20.

$30 \div 5 = 6$ The quotient is 6.

PAGE 123

$4\overline{)32} = 8$ $4\overline{)12} = 3$ $2\overline{)14} = 7$

$5\overline{)20} = 4$ $3\overline{)27} = 9$ $5\overline{)25} = 5$

PAGE 124

$14 \div 7 = 2$	$18 \div 6 = 3$	$30 \div 6 = 5$
$6 \div 6 = 1$	$35 \div 7 = 5$	$54 \div 6 = 9$
$24 \div 6 = 4$	$12 \div 6 = 2$	$7 \div 7 = 1$
$28 \div 7 = 4$	$42 \div 6 = 7$	$21 \div 7 = 3$

$6\overline{)24} = 4$ $6\overline{)36} = 6$ $7\overline{)56} = 8$

$6\overline{)48} = 8$ $7\overline{)42} = 6$ $7\overline{)63} = 9$

$7\overline{)49} = 7$ $7\overline{)70} = 10$ $6\overline{)60} = 10$

PAGE 125

$40 \div 8 = 5$	$16 \div 8 = 2$	$27 \div 9 = 3$
$72 \div 9 = 8$	$24 \div 8 = 3$	$9 \div 9 = 1$
$90 \div 9 = 10$	$45 \div 9 = 5$	$32 \div 8 = 4$
$8 \div 8 = 1$	$18 \div 9 = 2$	$48 \div 8 = 6$

$9\overline{)36} = 4$ $8\overline{)56} = 7$ $9\overline{)81} = 9$

$9\overline{)63} = 7$ $8\overline{)80} = 10$ $8\overline{)32} = 4$

$8\overline{)64} = 8$ $9\overline{)54} = 6$ $8\overline{)72} = 9$

PAGE 126

$27 \div 9 = 3$	$18 \div 6 = 3$	$45 \div 9 = 5$
$28 \div 7 = 4$	$9 \div 9 = 1$	$30 \div 6 = 5$
$16 \div 8 = 2$	$42 \div 6 = 7$	$32 \div 8 = 4$
$54 \div 6 = 9$	$35 \div 7 = 5$	$12 \div 6 = 2$
$24 \div 8 = 3$	$40 \div 8 = 5$	$72 \div 9 = 8$
$24 \div 6 = 4$	$18 \div 9 = 2$	$21 \div 7 = 3$
$80 \div 8 = 10$	$14 \div 7 = 2$	$48 \div 8 = 6$

PAGE 127

$7\overline{)42} = 6$ $6\overline{)60} = 10$ $7\overline{)35} = 5$

$6\overline{)30} = 5$ $8\overline{)72} = 9$ $9\overline{)54} = 6$

$9\overline{)18} = 2$ $7\overline{)21} = 3$ $8\overline{)24} = 3$

$6\overline{)48} = 8$ $9\overline{)45} = 5$ $8\overline{)40} = 5$

$7\overline{)63} = 9$ $7\overline{)14} = 2$ $9\overline{)81} = 9$

$9\overline{)27} = 3$ $6\overline{)18} = 3$ $7\overline{)49} = 7$

PAGE 128

54	9
36	6
18	3
30	5
48	8
42	7

21	3
56	8
28	4
35	5
70	10
42	6

40	5
72	9
8	1
16	2
24	3
64	8

90	10
18	2
45	5
81	9
63	7
36	4

PAGE 129

START

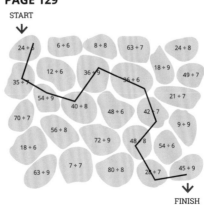

FINISH

PAGE 130

6 tickets

5 plates

8 squares

7 cars

$2

PAGE 131

$20 \div 10 = 2$	$50 \div 10 = 5$	$70 \div 10 = 7$

$10\overline{)40} = 4$ $10\overline{)80} = 8$ $10\overline{)10} = 1$

$10\overline{)90} = 9$ $10\overline{)30} = 3$ $10\overline{)60} = 6$

$30 \div 10 = 3$	$100 \div 10 = 10$	$40 \div 10 = 4$

$10\overline{)60} = 6$ $10\overline{)90} = 9$ $10\overline{)20} = 2$

$10\overline{)70} = 7$ $10\overline{)50} = 5$ $10\overline{)80} = 8$

PAGE 132

$250 \div 5 = 50$	$240 \div 3 = 80$	$160 \div 2 = 80$
$320 \div 8 = 40$	$360 \div 4 = 90$	$720 \div 9 = 80$
$210 \div 7 = 30$	$480 \div 8 = 60$	$540 \div 6 = 90$
$270 \div 9 = 30$	$350 \div 5 = 70$	$450 \div 9 = 50$

PAGE 133

$3,600 \div 6 = 600$

$1,400 \div 2 = 700$

$12,000 \div 4 = 3,000$

$160,000 \div 8 = 20,000$

$810,000 \div 9 = 90,000$

$30,000,000 \div 5 = 6,000,000$

PAGE 134

$3 \div 1 = 3$	$9 \div 1 = 9$
$6 \div 6 = 1$	$2 \div 2 = 1$
$10 \div 1 = 10$	$5 \div 1 = 5$
$2 \div 1 = 2$	$3 \div 3 = 1$
$8 \div 8 = 1$	$6 \div 1 = 6$
$10 \div 10 = 1$	$9 \div 9 = 1$
$4 \div 4 = 1$	$7 \div 1 = 7$
$8 \div 1 = 8$	$1 \div 1 = 1$
$7 \div 7 = 1$	$5 \div 5 = 1$

Any number divided by 1 is that same number. Any number divided by itself is 1.

Answer key

PAGE 135

0 ÷ 2 = 0   0 ÷ 8 = 0

0 ÷ 10 = 0   0 ÷ 5 = 0

0 ÷ 6 = 0   0 ÷ 1 = 0

0 ÷ 3 = 0   0 ÷ 9 = 0

0 ÷ 7 = 0   0 ÷ 4 = 0

0 ÷ 16 = 0   0 ÷ 28 = 0

0 ÷ 47 = 0   0 ÷ 93 = 0

PAGE 136

24 ÷ 12 = 2   55 ÷ 11 = 5   48 ÷ 12 = 4

77 ÷ 11 = 7   72 ÷ 12 = 6   22 ÷ 11 = 2

33 ÷ 11 = 3   121 ÷ 11 = 11   96 ÷ 12 = 8

60 ÷ 12 = 5   108 ÷ 12 = 9   88 ÷ 11 = 8

$11\overline{)44}$ = 4 $11\overline{)66}$ = 6 $12\overline{)144}$ = 12

$12\overline{)36}$ = 3 $12\overline{)84}$ = 7 $11\overline{)99}$ = 9

$12\overline{)96}$ = 8 $11\overline{)110}$ = 10 $12\overline{)48}$ = 4

$12\overline{)120}$ = 10 $11\overline{)33}$ = 3

PAGE 137

36 ÷ 12 = 3   132 ÷ 11 = 12   72 ÷ 12 = 6

108 ÷ 12 = 9   55 ÷ 11 = 5   88 ÷ 11 = 8

110 ÷ 11 = 10   24 ÷ 12 = 2   84 ÷ 12 = 7

$11\overline{)77}$ = 7 $12\overline{)48}$ = 4 $11\overline{)33}$ = 3

$11\overline{)22}$ = 2 $12\overline{)120}$ = 10 $12\overline{)12}$ = 1

$12\overline{)60}$ = 5 $11\overline{)44}$ = 4 $11\overline{)99}$ = 9

$12\overline{)132}$ = 11

PAGE 138

25 ÷ 5 = 5   21 ÷ 7 = 3   24 ÷ 3 = 8

42 ÷ 6 = 7   32 ÷ 8 = 4   15 ÷ 3 = 5

24 ÷ 4 = 6   55 ÷ 11 = 5   63 ÷ 7 = 9

30 ÷ 6 = 5   64 ÷ 8 = 8   45 ÷ 9 = 5

72 ÷ 12 = 6   16 ÷ 2 = 8   56 ÷ 7 = 8

35 ÷ 5 = 7   27 ÷ 3 = 9   36 ÷ 6 = 6

108 ÷ 12 = 9   70 ÷ 7 = 10   28 ÷ 7 = 4

PAGE 139

$12\overline{)132}$ = 11 $7\overline{)42}$ = 6 $5\overline{)20}$ = 4

$4\overline{)28}$ = 7 $9\overline{)81}$ = 9 $4\overline{)32}$ = 8

$9\overline{)72}$ = 8 $3\overline{)21}$ = 7 $8\overline{)40}$ = 5

$7\overline{)49}$ = 7 $11\overline{)121}$ = 11 $5\overline{)50}$ = 10

$12\overline{)96}$ = 8 $8\overline{)56}$ = 7 $9\overline{)54}$ = 6

PAGE 140

24 ÷ 6	16 ÷ 4	48 ÷ 8		84 ÷ 12	33 ÷ 3	55 ÷ 5
70 ÷ 7	40 ÷ 10	24 ÷ 2		56 ÷ 8	49 ÷ 7	77 ÷ 11
28 ÷ 4	81 ÷ 9	32 ÷ 8		32 ÷ 4	56 ÷ 7	40 ÷ 4

42 ÷ 7	24 ÷ 4	20 ÷ 4		40 ÷ 5	30 ÷ 3	60 ÷ 12
60 ÷ 12	35 ÷ 7	16 ÷ 2		90 ÷ 9	60 ÷ 6	20 ÷ 4
40 ÷ 8	55 ÷ 11	30 ÷ 10		100 ÷ 10	70 ÷ 7	30 ÷ 5

36 ÷ 3	60 ÷ 5	27 ÷ 3
84 ÷ 7	72 ÷ 6	45 ÷ 5
108 ÷ 9	36 ÷ 6	48 ÷ 8

PAGE 141

6 orders

3 lemonades

5 cheese pizzas

PAGE 142

3 × 5 = 15   7 × 11 = 77   33 ÷ 3 = 11

14 ÷ 7 = 2   1 × 6 = 6   4 ÷ 1 = 4

11 × 10 = 110   30 ÷ 5 = 6   7 × 8 = 56

45 ÷ 9 = 5   12 × 2 = 24   5 × 3 = 15

20 ÷ 2 = 10   30 ÷ 10 = 3   9 × 6 = 54

36 ÷ 6 = 6   8 × 6 = 48   27 ÷ 9 = 3

48 ÷ 4 = 12   3 × 7 = 21   10 × 5 = 50

32 ÷ 4 = 8   4 × 9 = 36   84 ÷ 12 = 7

PAGE 143

2 × 9 = 18   35 ÷ 5 = 7   7 × 7 = 49

48 ÷ 6 = 8   12 × 7 = 84   9 × 3 = 27

81 ÷ 9 = 9   5 × 4 = 20   40 ÷ 8 = 5

8 × 8 = 64   28 ÷ 4 = 7   36 ÷ 9 = 4

18 ÷ 3 = 6   12 × 12 = 144   90 ÷ 10 = 9

5 × 5 = 25   12 ÷ 3 = 4   6 × 7 = 42

11 × 11 = 121   8 × 9 = 72   30 ÷ 6 = 5

16 ÷ 2 = 8   3 × 11 = 33   16 ÷ 8 = 2

PAGE 144

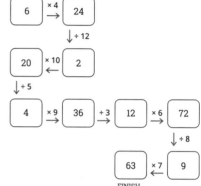

PAGE 145

66 ÷ 6 = 11   24 ÷ 3 = 8

2 × 5 = 10   60 ÷ 5 = 12

5 × 1 = 5   6 × 10 = 60

40 ÷ 10 = 4   2 × 3 = 6

7 × 11 = 77   4 × 7 = 28

9 × 8 = 72   10 ÷ 5 = 2

10 ÷ 2 = 5   12 × 8 = 96

4 × 9 = 36   54 ÷ 9 = 6

12 ÷ 4 = 3   3 × 9 = 27

49 ÷ 7 = 7   36 ÷ 3 = 12

PAGE 146

3 + 5 = 8   24 − 6 = 18   9 × 3 = 27

100 ÷ 10 = 10   6 × 7 = 42   9 + 12 = 21

21 − 7 = 14   45 ÷ 5 = 9   90 − 9 = 81

11 × 12 = 132   12 + 11 = 23   36 ÷ 4 = 9

64 − 8 = 56   8 × 3 = 24   5 + 6 = 11

20 ÷ 4 = 5   12 × 4 = 48   50 ÷ 10 = 5

35 + 7 = 42   32 − 8 = 24   6 × 6 = 36

27 − 9 = 18   54 ÷ 9 = 6   12 × 6 = 72

PAGE 147

$2 \times 11 = 22$	$5 + 10 = 15$	$72 \div 6 = 12$
$11 - 7 = 4$	$4 \times 4 = 16$	$7 + 5 = 12$
$9 + 8 = 17$	$12 - 7 = 5$	$18 \div 6 = 3$
$4 \times 9 = 36$	$49 \div 7 = 7$	$10 - 6 = 4$
$6 + 6 = 12$	$48 \div 6 = 8$	$3 \times 3 = 9$
$9 \times 12 = 108$	$20 - 10 = 10$	$44 \div 11 = 4$
$45 + 9 = 54$	$21 \div 3 = 7$	$18 - 2 = 16$
$48 - 12 = 36$	$7 \times 7 = 49$	$100 \div 10 = 10$

PAGE 148

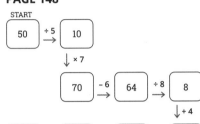

PAGE 149

4 and 9

72

8 and 3

2

50 and 5

5

3 and 6

PAGE 150

$34

45 books

43 points

4 sour gummies

PAGE 151

24 tickets

26 tickets

21 tickets

Charlotte will have 10 tickets. Here are some possible way she could spend those tickets:
the Ferris wheel and the giant slide
the bumper cars and the giant slide
the flying swings and the fun house

PAGE 152

 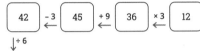

PAGE 153

Answers may vary. Some possible answers are shown below.

PAGE 154

fourths	sixths	halves
eighths	fourths	thirds

PAGE 155

$\frac{2}{4}$	$\frac{4}{6}$
$\frac{1}{2}$	$\frac{2}{3}$
$\frac{1}{4}$	$\frac{6}{8}$

PAGE 156

$\frac{1}{4}$	$\frac{2}{3}$
$\frac{3}{6}$	$\frac{4}{6}$

PAGE 157

$\frac{3}{4}$

$\frac{5}{8}$

$\frac{1}{3}$

PAGE 158

$\frac{1}{2}$	$\frac{4}{8}$	$\frac{3}{6}$
$\frac{1}{4}$	$\frac{2}{3}$	$\frac{3}{6}$
$\frac{2}{6}$		
$\frac{1}{4}$		

PAGE 159

Shading patterns may vary. Some possible answers are shown below.

PAGE 160

Drawings may vary. Some possible answers are shown below.

Answer key

PAGE 161

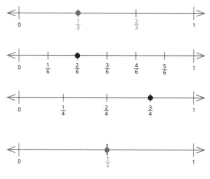

PAGE 162

$\frac{5}{6}$

$\frac{1}{4}$

Answers may vary. Some possible answers are shown below.

$\frac{3}{6}$

$\frac{2}{3}$

PAGE 163

$\frac{4}{8}$

$\frac{3}{8}$

$\frac{2}{6}$

$\frac{2}{3}$

$\frac{3}{4}$

PAGE 164

$\frac{4}{4}$ $\qquad$ $\frac{2}{2}$

$\frac{8}{8}$ $\qquad$ $\frac{6}{6}$

When you divide the numerator by the denominator, you get 1.

PAGE 165

$\frac{1}{3} < \frac{2}{3}$ $\qquad$ $\frac{3}{6} < \frac{5}{6}$ $\qquad$ $\frac{7}{8} > \frac{3}{8}$

$\frac{2}{4} = \frac{2}{4}$ $\qquad$ $\frac{1}{6} < \frac{2}{6}$ $\qquad$ $\frac{2}{8} < \frac{5}{8}$

$\frac{1}{4} < \frac{2}{4}$ $\qquad$ $\frac{5}{6} > \frac{4}{6}$ $\qquad$ $\frac{3}{4} > \frac{1}{4}$

PAGE 166

$\frac{1}{8} < \frac{1}{3}$ $\qquad$ $\frac{1}{2} > \frac{1}{4}$

$\frac{1}{4} < \frac{1}{3}$ $\qquad$ $\frac{1}{3} > \frac{1}{6}$

$\frac{1}{6} > \frac{1}{8}$ $\qquad$ $\frac{1}{6} < \frac{1}{4}$

$\frac{1}{8} < \frac{1}{2}$ $\qquad$ $\frac{1}{4} > \frac{1}{8}$

PAGE 167

$\frac{3}{8} < \frac{3}{4}$ $\qquad$ $\frac{5}{8} < \frac{5}{6}$

$\frac{2}{3} > \frac{2}{8}$ $\qquad$ $\frac{4}{6} > \frac{4}{8}$

$\frac{3}{4} > \frac{3}{6}$ $\qquad$ $\frac{2}{4} < \frac{2}{3}$

PAGE 168

$\frac{1}{6} < \frac{1}{4}$ $\qquad$ $\frac{1}{2} > \frac{1}{3}$

$\frac{2}{6} < \frac{3}{6}$ $\qquad$ $\frac{3}{4} > \frac{1}{4}$

$\frac{4}{8} < \frac{4}{6}$ $\qquad$ $\frac{2}{4} < \frac{2}{3}$

$\frac{2}{3} > \frac{1}{3}$ $\qquad$ $\frac{2}{6} = \frac{2}{6}$

Answers may vary. Some possible answers are shown below.

$\frac{1}{4} < \frac{2}{4}$ $\qquad$ $\frac{2}{6} < \frac{2}{3}$

$\frac{5}{8} > \frac{3}{8}$ $\qquad$ $\frac{1}{2} > \frac{1}{4}$

PAGE 169

Jenna read more.

Ashley ate more.

Carter walked a longer distance.

Riley ate more.

Audrey ate more. She had less popcorn left over.

PAGE 170

Shading patterns may vary. Some possible answers are shown below.

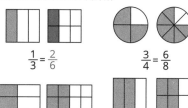

$\frac{1}{3} = \frac{2}{6}$ $\qquad\qquad$ $\frac{3}{4} = \frac{6}{8}$

$\frac{2}{4} = \frac{4}{8}$ $\qquad\qquad$ $\frac{2}{3} = \frac{4}{6}$

PAGE 171

Shading patterns may vary. Some possible answers are shown below.

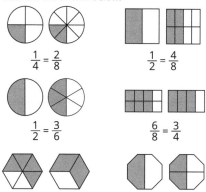

$\frac{1}{4} = \frac{2}{8}$ $\qquad\qquad$ $\frac{1}{2} = \frac{4}{8}$

$\frac{1}{2} = \frac{3}{6}$ $\qquad\qquad$ $\frac{6}{8} = \frac{3}{4}$

$\frac{4}{6} = \frac{2}{3}$ $\qquad\qquad$ $\frac{1}{2} = \frac{2}{4}$

PAGE 172

Shading patterns may vary. Some possible answers are shown below.

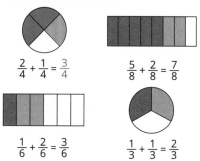

$\frac{2}{4} + \frac{1}{4} = \frac{3}{4}$ $\qquad$ $\frac{5}{8} + \frac{2}{8} = \frac{7}{8}$

$\frac{1}{6} + \frac{2}{6} = \frac{3}{6}$ $\qquad$ $\frac{1}{3} + \frac{1}{3} = \frac{2}{3}$

PAGE 173

Shading patterns may vary. Some possible answers are shown below.

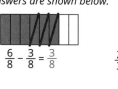

$\frac{6}{8} - \frac{3}{8} = \frac{3}{8}$ $\qquad$ $\frac{2}{3} - \frac{1}{3} = \frac{1}{3}$

$\frac{4}{6} - \frac{1}{6} = \frac{3}{6}$ $\qquad$ $\frac{3}{4} - \frac{2}{4} = \frac{1}{4}$

223

PAGE 174

51¢	37¢
58¢	55¢
77¢	92¢

PAGE 175

$2.12	$7.45
$11.00	$8.46
$11.82	

PAGE 176

$62
$35
$40
$10

PAGE 177

$715
$300
$880
$40

PAGE 178

$1.40 + $3.50 $4.90	$8.70 − $6.30 $2.40	$3.25 + $8.03 $11.28
$5.85 − $2.25 $3.60	$4.75 + $3.23 $7.98	$6.89 + $5.27 $12.16
$8.49 + $1.20 $9.69	$6.45 − $3.10 $3.35	$7.31 − $2.99 $4.32
	$7.75 + $4.95 $12.70	$8.06 − $4.39 $3.67

PAGE 179

$6.85
$1.21
$4.79
$8.75

PAGE 180

| 2:25 | 6:10 | 10:00 |
| 1:34 | 4:57 | 12:00 |

PAGE 181

PAGE 182

2 inches	4 inches
5 inches	
6 inches	

PAGE 183

7 centimeters	7 centimeters
12 centimeters	
5 centimeters	
14 centimeters	

PAGE 184

| 4 grams | 2 kilograms |
| 900 grams | 20 kilograms |

PAGE 185

| 15 milliliters | 4 liters |
| 300 liters | 700 milliliters |

PAGE 186

10 days
34 minutes
3 liters
10 kilograms

PAGE 187

4:48
2 liters
4 necklaces
40 minutes

PAGE 188

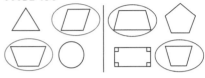

quadrilateral   hexagon   triangle

PAGE 189

octagon	quadrilateral	pentagon
hexagon	quadrilateral	pentagon
quadrilateral	octagon	

PAGE 190

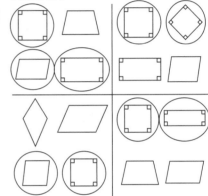

PAGE 191

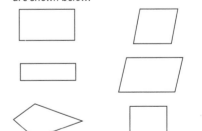

PAGE 192

Answers may vary. Some possible answers are shown below.

The last shape is a square.

PAGE 193

Answers may vary. Some possible answers are shown below.

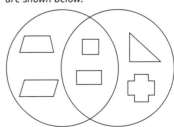

Answer key

PAGE 194

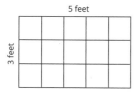

6 square feet

15 square feet

PAGE 195

10 square meters	30 square inches
36 square yards	63 square feet
24 square feet	21 square feet

PAGE 196

5 inches	3 meters
7 feet	8 yards
7 feet	4 feet

PAGE 197

33 square yards

40 square feet

PAGE 198

70 square feet

41 square feet

44 square feet

PAGE 199

22 inches	20 inches
13 centimeters	34 meters

PAGE 200

36 feet	22 centimeters
15 inches	48 meters
16 feet	30 feet

PAGE 201

3 inches	6 meters
4 centimeters	4 feet
5 centimeters	7 feet

PAGE 202

Perimeter = 18 inches
Area = 18 square inches

Perimeter = 12 inches
Area = 9 square inches

PAGE 203

34 yards

72 square feet

4 feet

3 feet

16 feet

PAGE 204

$690

24 square meters

12 meters

PAGE 205

10 meters

9 packets

Answers may vary. One possible answer is shown below.

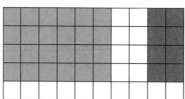

18 square meters

6 bags

PAGE 206

93 cans

152 cans

14 cans

PAGE 207

5 boxes

6 cans

Ms. Acosta's class

5 cans

Mr. Maben's class on Thursday

PAGE 208

$180

$820

$320

$500

PAGE 209

$140

$90

$30

$47